Marguerite Pramann

Marching Through

Immanuel's Ground

The Evangelical Church on the Minnesota Prairie

by Lorraine Esterly Pierce

RLE PRESS
East Lansing, Michigan

Marching Through Immanuel's Ground:
The Evangelical Church on the Minnesota Prairie

Copyright © 1999 by Lorraine Esterly Pierce

Published by RLE Press
P.O. Box 732
East Lansing, Michigan 48826
Books may be ordered from the above address.

Library of Congress Catalog Card Number: 99-74246
ISBN 0-9672527-0-9

Printed in the United States of America

"*Remember the days of old, consider the years of many generations: ask thy father, and he will show thee; thy elders, and they will tell thee.*"

Deuteronomy 32:7

To My Evangelical Forebears in Minnesota

Great-grandparents Gottfried (1824-1908) and Ottilie Guderian (1838-1900) Oesterle, who came to the United States from Germany in 1859, farmed, and were early members of Maple Grove Immanuel Evangelical Church;

Great-grandmother Anna Sterck Diettert Weier (1840-1918) who came to the United States from Germany in 1884, was a mid-wife, and was a member of Hanover Zion Evangelical Church;

Grandparents Henry (1865-1945) and Emma Diettert (1873-1961) Esterly, who farmed and were members of the Hanover Zion Evangelical Church;

Parents Reverend Ralph (1906-1958) and Alberta Marckhoff (1910-1987) Esterly who served in the ministry at Duluth Chester Park Evangelical, Winona Immanuel Evangelical, Wells Salem and Dunbar Zion Evangelical United Brethren, and St. Paul Faith Evangelical United Brethren Churches.

FOREWORD

Former Speaker of the House Tip O'Neil once observed that "All politics is local." It can also be said that "All church history is local."

Lorraine Esterly Pierce's book, *Marching Through Immanuel's Ground*, is a study of church history but is not about historic Church Councils, or the founding of major denominations or the growth of American mega-churches, but centers on the struggles and heartaches of twenty-two small local churches in southwestern Minnesota over the past 150 years.

Their background was German pietism with an emphasis on a personal experience with Christ through conversion, holy living, personal integrity, love of neighbor and a close fellowship with each other. They were called the "Evangelische Gemeinschaft" (Fellowship/Association) or the "Evangelical Church." Their stance was not to be conformed to this world or what Richard Niebuhr termed, "Christ Versus Culture."

After years of careful research and personally interviewing members from both closed and surviving churches, Lorraine Esterly Pierce has identified herself with their painful struggles, as this is also her religious heritage.

These early pioneers endured many hardships, the most dramatic being the Dakota Conflict in which many Evangelicals, other white settlers and Native Americans lost their lives.

One of the major adjustments which these churches faced was the transition from the German to the English language in their worship, accelerated by some of the anti-German hysteria of World War I. The stately German hymns and what some consider to be the finest translation of the New Testament – Martin Luther's – were difficult to relinquish.

Another major adjustment was the migration in Minnesota from rural to urban areas, especially the Twin Cities. As farms became larger and the young people left for the cities some churches diminished in size and had to close. This was very painful for the older generation. Probably the most painful and frustrating adjustment of these rural and small town churches was the 1968 merger of the Evangelical United Brethren Church with the Methodist Church. The earlier union between the Evangelical and the United Brethren Churches in 1946 was less traumatic as it united two denominations of about the same size.

Many of the members of these churches felt that they had no voice in this decision and that it had been forced on them by the hierarchy. They felt that they were "swallowed up" by a much larger and more politicized denomination.

In some ways this book is more than a history. It is a psychological insight into the sense of helplessness many people feel today in our society where the individual is powerless and our destiny is taken over by powers beyond our control.

Lorraine Esterly Pierce has made a real contribution to our sympathetic understanding of the "little people" who have gone through "trial and tribulation" and whose voice has not been heard.

Kenneth W. Krueger

Former Editor of Adult Publications
Otterbein Press, Dayton, Ohio

TABLE OF CONTENTS

Photographs of Churches in Study Areas
(between pages 106 and 107)

The Evangelical Churches in South Central Minnesota

Church	Photo Number
Dunbar Zion	1
Wells Salem	2, 3, 4
Rice Lake Emmanuel	5, 6, 7, 8
Brush Creek Tabor	9
Blue Earth Immanuel	10, 11, 12
Blue Earth Salem	13, 14, 15, 16

The Evangelical Churches in Southwestern Minnesota

Church	Photo Number
Fairmont Salem	17
Welcome Emmanuel	18, 19
Worthington Emmanuel	20, 21
Luverne Ebenezer (Pleasant View)	22, 23, 24
Steen Salem	25
Pipestone Salem	26
Pipestone Zion	27, 28
Hendricks Zion (New Grove)	29, 30
Clifton Bethel	31
Marshall Salem	32, 33

The Evangelical Churches in Western Minnesota

Church	Photo Number
Madison Ebenezer	34, 35
Bellingham Zion	36, 37, 38
Salem (Yellowbank Township)	39
Yellowbank Emmanuel	40
Odessa Salem	41
Fairfield Zion	42

PREFACE

This book, *Marching Through Immanuel's Ground: The Evangelical Church on the Minnesota Prairie*, is the result of a life-long fascination with "the Days of Old" and an early interest in Evangelicals in Minnesota. Growing up in Evangelical parsonages in Minnesota, in the 1950s I came across Albert H. Utzinger's *History of the Minnesota Conference of the Evangelical Association: 1856 to 1922*. This early Evangelical history fascinated me, and I remember commenting to my father that since Utzinger's book only went to 1922, someone needed to write the more recent history. He replied that perhaps I could and should do that when I grew up. Clearly this book is not that monumental in scope, but it is an attempt to bring some of that history up to date.

When I came back to the idea after many years (about forty!) I decided to interview people from some of the old Evangelical churches in Minnesota and then study other aspects of these churches' history. Clearly I could not cover all of the old Evangelical churches, so I decided to concentrate on churches in three areas which were representative of the Evangelical Church with its primarily rural and small town base.

The three areas selected - south central, southwestern and western Minnesota (see map, page xxiii) - contained twenty-two Evangelical churches which had been in existence in 1922. They ranged from small rural churches on the open prairie, to fairly large churches in small towns, to smaller churches in larger towns. Other areas in Minnesota – such as that around Paynesville/Lake Koronis, (see map, page xxiii) which is often referred to as the cradle of Minnesota Evangelicalism – would also have been valuable to study. I only wish I could have studied all of the Minnesota Evangelical/Evangelical United Brethren churches.

Marching Through Immanuel's Ground does not focus only on the history of the churches in the three areas studied. Rather, it is the story of the Evangelical Church in Minnesota using the history of the selected churches to illustrate this account. Relevant perspectives from the national and state level are included, as is information on the economic and social conditions of the times.

The major reasons for doing this study are not only to help preserve part of a past that may soon be largely lost, but also to look at and think about what that part of the past meant and what it might mean to us today. Thus, these churches and the Evangelicals in Minnesota were studied in the context of such questions as:

- Who were the Evangelicals and what was important to them?
- How did the Evangelicals remain true to their faith and convictions, and yet continue to be relevant to the times; i.e., to "be in the world but not of it"?

- How did Minnesota Evangelicals confront and respond to major issues such as the German to English language change?
- How did the Evangelicals feel about and respond to the 1946 union with the United Brethren, creating the Evangelical United Brethren Church?
- How did the E.U.B.'s respond to the post-World War II population shift from rural to urban areas in Minnesota?
- How did the E.U.B.'s perceive and react to the 1968 merger with the Methodists, resulting in the United Methodist Church?
- And finally, what remains of the Evangelical heritage and the faith that gave it meaning, and how can it be preserved?

There are undoubtedly some errors that have gone undetected, regarding dates, tables and other factual information. I have done my best to double check all information, but would ask the reader to heed the request made by Albert H. Utzinger in his *History of the Minnesota Conference: 1856 to 1922*, when he stated:

> Some of the dates and other facts may be incorrect, but we endeavored to get as near to them as possible. If any of our readers discover mistakes, think the information correctly, and read on, remembering that we are human, and did the best we could under the circumstances.

In a work of this nature historical facts are recounted, but more importantly, issues are raised and perceptions given that are sensitive and sometimes provocative in nature. I take full responsibility for how these issues and perceptions are presented, and hope the reader – whether former Evangelical, Evangelical United Brethren, Methodist, United Methodist or "interested bystander" – will read this study of the Evangelical Church in Minnesota with a mind and heart open to this particular understanding of a past both worthy of preservation and still capable of making contributions today and in the future.

Lorraine Esterly Pierce
East Lansing, Michigan

Acknowledgements

This book was written with the help of many people. My thanks are due to all of them, starting with my husband Howard. He has shepherded the manuscript through all the trials and tribulations that publishing a book entails, and having been raised as a Methodist with no knowledge of Evangelicals or E.U.B.'s until adulthood, he is now more than a little familiar with their history in Minnesota. He encouraged me to continue work on the book when I became discouraged, because he understood how much it meant to me to complete this project; I could not have finished it without his support.

My thanks go also to Thelma Boeder, Archivist, Minnesota Annual Conference, United Methodist Church. Thelma was not only extremely helpful in providing the old church records, photographs and other valuable research materials; she gave me much food for thought and shared her enthusiasm and expertise unstintingly.

Dr. Kenneth Krueger, former Editor of Adult Publications, Otterbein Press, and currently Pastor Emeritus, Fairview United Methodist Church in Dayton, Ohio, edited the manuscript chapter by chapter. I can not thank him enough for his ever-gracious willingness to share his perspectives with me.

Kai Mitchell not only did layout work, but provided much other valuable assistance on the myriad details of publishing a book. Also, I want to thank artist Tim Liess for allowing me to use his beautiful painting, *Our Father,* for the cover of the book.

Tim is an Indiana artist whose pastoral landscapes truly capture the light of a prairie sky as seen in *Our Father.*

Special thanks are due to those who opened their homes to me, drove me to interviews, churches, cemeteries, etc. I began the research in Wells where I had lived from 1942 to 1952, from age one to eleven. I stayed with Irene Bebler, who baby-sat with me fifty years earlier, and she made me feel right at home again. We went to see the old Dunbar Zion Church (jointly served with Wells Salem), which is now a farm storage building. Even in its present condition, it evoked memories of the Autumn harvest services there in the 1940s and singing "Come, Ye Thankful People, Come," amidst the bounty of the earth.

As I moved westward, I continued to be overwhelmed by the warmth and hospitality that were shown to me, and also by the willingness of people to go out of their way to help arrange interviews and give me access to written records. People willingly shared their history and their perspectives on that history, and working with these people made doing the research a joy.

Special mention should be made here of Helen and Herb Reko (Blue Earth Immanuel), Shirley Unke (Fairmont), Vivian and Clarence Erbes (Worthington Emmanuel), Lorraine Draper (Pipestone Peace), Elzora Ott (Luverne), and Lillian Wendland (Bellingham Zion).

There were many others - both lay people and clergy - that I interviewed from the churches in the three study areas. All of these people (hopefully I have not inadvertently left out any names) are listed in the Bibliography, and I thank them for their time and contributions to the study.

Special thanks also go to Verdell and Larry Blokzyl, who hosted a wonderful get-together that included several former E.U.B., now mostly retired United Methodist ministers, and their spouses. I also want to thank Bea Johnson, LaVerne Mitby, Russ Scheffer, Joe Amato, Pat Breidenbach, Jim Simmons, Mary Bakeman, Robert Friedrich, Glenn Offerman, Paul Daniels, Glenn Esterly, Harry Heitke, Luverne Liebrenz, and Randall Pemberton for their assistance.

Inspiration for the book's title, *Marching Through Immanuel's Ground* – part of the fourth verse of the well known hymn "We're Marching to Zion" – came while singing that hymn at Salem Church near Paynesville in April 1997. The service there was part of the excellent program arranged by Pearl Heitke for the meeting of the United Methodist Historical Society of Minnesota. While Salem was officially closed some thirty years ago, it is now undergoing restoration, and holds Christmas services and the summer Salemfest. Thus, as Salem's past is celebrated, so too her witness continues.

And finally, I am grateful for the opportunity to tell the story of a heritage and tradition which held me in its circle and still gives meaning and direction to my life.

Lorraine Esterly Pierce

Location of Churches in Study Areas

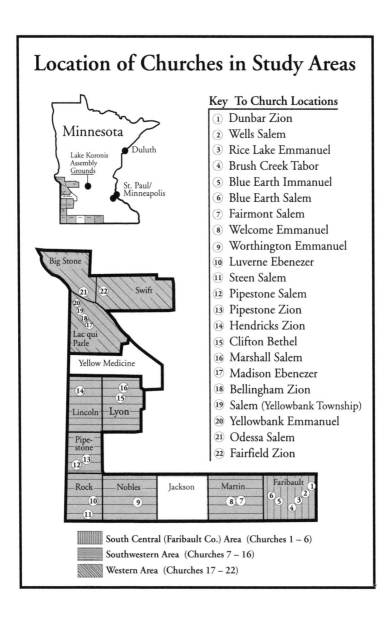

Key To Church Locations

1. Dunbar Zion
2. Wells Salem
3. Rice Lake Emmanuel
4. Brush Creek Tabor
5. Blue Earth Immanuel
6. Blue Earth Salem
7. Fairmont Salem
8. Welcome Emmanuel
9. Worthington Emmanuel
10. Luverne Ebenezer
11. Steen Salem
12. Pipestone Salem
13. Pipestone Zion
14. Hendricks Zion
15. Clifton Bethel
16. Marshall Salem
17. Madison Ebenezer
18. Bellingham Zion
19. Salem (Yellowbank Township)
20. Yellowbank Emmanuel
21. Odessa Salem
22. Fairfield Zion

Minnesota

Lake Koronis Assembly Grounds

Duluth

St. Paul/ Minneapolis

Big Stone

Swift

Lac qui Parle

Yellow Medicine

Lincoln   Lyon

Pipe-stone

Rock   Nobles   Jackson   Martin   Faribault

South Central (Faribault Co.) Area (Churches 1 – 6)

Southwestern Area (Churches 7 – 16)

Western Area (Churches 17 – 22)

Chapter One

A New Church in a New Country

The Evangelical Church founded by Jacob Albright and the United Brethren Church founded by Phillip Otterbein both began in Pennsylvania in about 1800. Their mission was to reach the German immigrants who were not receiving the gospel in their own language ...

Introduction

This statement which I and many others memorized as part of Evangelical United Brethren catechism, says a lot in a few words. This chapter will try to put flesh on this bare-bones statement, and will look at the beginnings of the Evangelical Church and also at the United Brethren and Methodists with whom they had much in common. This is not intended to be an historical or theological treatise, but simply an introduction to the Evangelicals before they followed new German immigrants across the country and into Minnesota.

The Times

The last quarter of the eighteenth century was a time of great change in many places, and nowhere more so than in the newly-formed United States of America. The Revolutionary War which resulted in the new independent nation brought increases in freedom and responsibility to citizens in the thirteen states. It did not result in a great increase in religious activity, however. In fact, as Paul Eller states, this was an era when people "...stood aside from organized religion. In 1800, 6.9 percent of the people were related to organized religion."[1] And K. James Stein calls this time "an age of unbelief" and states that "The moral depression concomitant with all wars made its devastating impact on the new nation."[2] Excessive drinking and the loosening of moral codes were on the increase, as is wont to occur in times of rapid societal change.

United Brethren Beginnings

There were those, however, who sought to rekindle some of the religious fervor that had been evident in the revival called the "Great Awakening" of the mid-eighteenth century. One of these was Phillip Otterbein (1726-1813) who had been educated in and came out of the Reformed Church in Germany. He was also greatly influenced by the German pietistic movement which stressed real religious commitment. As Eller puts it:

The core of religion was held to be life committed to God, not baptism nor assent to creed. Bible reading, confession, free prayer, hymn singing, testimony - these were the avenues to achieve an active, biblical faith.[3]

Otterbein came to what were then the British colonies in 1752. While he remained officially in his Reformed Church and served Reformed congregations in Maryland and Pennsylvania, the last church he served (in Baltimore) was semi-independent and took the name "The German Evangelical Reformed Church."

Otterbein met others of like persuasion in his evangelistic and ministerial work, among whom were Martin Boehm and Francis Asbury. Martin Boehm (1725-1812) was born into a German-speaking Mennonite family in Pennsylvania, and was chosen by lot (a Mennonite tradition) to be his church's pastor. He was then led to a more committed religious faith, and began preaching in other German-speaking communities. It was near Lancaster, Pennsylvania that Boehm was preaching at Pentecost 1767 and Otterbein heard him preach; after the meeting Otterbein clasped Boehm's hand and exclaimed "Wir sind Bruder!" ("We are brothers!").

It would be many years before the real organization of the United Brethren in Christ would grow out of this meeting and recognition of shared beliefs and faith. By the last decade of the eighteenth century, Otterbein, Boehm and some others of like mind and faith were moving toward a more distinct organized fellowship. In 1800 the group resolved to meet on an annual basis and Otterbein and Boehm (who had been expelled by the

Mennonites in 1780) were elected as leaders. There was still much resistance to official structure, however. As Eller states:

> The transition from movement to organization was effected slowly and not without continued and firm opposition. The pronounced increase of the Mennonite element in the movement after 1800, which eclipsed the German Reformed element, retarded endeavors at organization. In 1802 by a decisive majority the proposal to draft and keep membership rolls was repudiated: few showed any concern for discipline, creed, ordination and the like.[4]

Oddly enough, it was one of Mennonite background, Christian Newcomer (1749-1830), who encouraged and brought structure and organization to the United Brethren. He pushed for a discipline and rule book. But most of the Mennonite group opposed this, holding that God's Word was sufficient. Newcomer also organized classes, and eventually others moved in this direction also. Newcomer was officially ordained by Otterbein with the assistance of a Methodist minister in 1813, and a discipline was finally adopted in 1817.

It should be noted that there were close associations between these early United Brethren and the early Methodists in this country during these years. As will be discussed further in the next section, Otterbein and Asbury were good friends and colleagues and there was much in common between the two groups. In fact, there was some discussion of and movement toward more unity and eventual union of the two groups, but this did not take place.

4

Early American Methodism

The first Methodists to come to the American colonies arrived in 1766,[5] but the Methodist movement itself began in England more than thirty years earlier. John Wesley (1703-1791), an Anglican (Church of England) priest, was led to preach of God's grace and salvation by faith and began an evangelistic ministry with others of similar convictions, including his brother Charles. They encountered much opposition from the organized church, but according to Maldwyn Edwards:

> All these attacks gave the Wesleys wide publicity and sympathy while stimulating the loyalty and devotion of their followers. The movement spread rapidly and societies were formed especially in the centers of population.[6]

By the 1840s the Methodists met in "class meetings;" they were not, however, a separate church at this time.

The Methodist movement that took root in the American colonies sought to minister to the English-speaking colonists. Francis Asbury (1745-1816), the most prominent Methodist minister and later bishop, came from England in 1771. Asbury was a tireless worker for the Methodist movement, and his associations extended to others who were engaged in similar work. He and Otterbein became close friends and it is clear that a deep mutual respect existed between the two great leaders. Asbury was also a colleague and friend of Martin Boehm's, and Boehm's son Henry became a Methodist minister who often traveled with Asbury.

At the time of the American Revolution the Methodist movement was still part of the Church of England. The definitive separation of Methodism as a distinct denomination did not take place until after Wesley's death in 1791. For all practical purposes, however, 1784 can be seen as the beginning of the Methodist Episcopal Church. At the Christmas Conference of 1784 Francis Asbury was ordained and named general superintendent, a title soon replaced by bishop.[7] Otterbein was one of the three who participated in Asbury's ordination.

The Methodist Episcopal Church (as its title indicates) chose to retain the episcopal (governed by bishops) system. Other aspects of governance were also put in place, such as the establishment of conferences, the itinerancy (whereby ministers were stationed on a charge by the bishop) and a discipline which outlined the beliefs and practices of the new Methodist Episcopal Church. The establishment of Methodism as a distinct denomination did not mean that early Methodist leaders such as Bishop Asbury did not continue to work with other like-minded movements. On the contrary, there continued to be much cooperation among them.

Evangelical Beginnings

The Evangelical movement, then Association, and later Church, originated in Pennsylvania in the late 1700s. Jacob Albrecht/Albright (1759-1808) was the American-born son of German immigrants; he was baptized and confirmed a Lutheran. He was a successful farmer and tile maker, but was not a happy man. As Bishop Milhouse then elaborates:

Jacob Albright was a very religious man, but was not satis-

6

fied with his early experience. After several of his children died of an epidemic, he was convinced that it was God's judgement upon him. In 1791, at a prayer meeting in the neighboring home of Adam Riegel, a United Brethren layman, he came into a new religious experience and assurance of the forgiving grace and transforming power of God.[8]

Albright then continued to associate with others of similar beliefs, and soon joined a Methodist class which met in a neighbor's home. Since this class was of course conducted in English, Albright worked hard to become more proficient in that language. He was granted an "exhorter's license" by the class, but was gradually led to the conviction that he should be preaching the gospel to his fellow Germans. By 1796 he had really become a full-time itinerant minister, traveling and preaching in parts of Pennsylvania, Maryland and Virginia.

Albright continued his association with the Methodists and with United Brethren as well. The development of the followers of Albright into a distinct and separate denomination was very gradual and Albright himself did not seem to be particularly interested in organizational structure.[9] By the early 1800s, the ministers and laypeople associated with Albright were simply known as "Albright's People," and in 1807 six months before his death in May 1808, they started to call themselves "The Newly-Formed Methodist Conference." That was changed in 1809 to the rather odd sounding name of "The So-Called Albright People."

These Evangelical Christians known as "The So-Called Albright People" then became much more organized in the next few years. One reason was that the new leaders after Albright's death, among whom was John Dreisbach, were more organizationally inclined and also saw more need for some organization as the group grew in size. Another reason was the development of a more clear-cut policy of the soon-to-be called Evangelical Association to concentrate on ministering almost exclusively to the German-speaking while the Methodists concentrated on those who spoke English.

One of the more definitive discussions on the language issue took place in 1810 between John Dreisbach and Francis Asbury. Asbury was very interested in having Dreisbach unite with the Methodists and to become fluent enough in English that he could then preach in both languages. Dreisbach then responded to this offer as follows:

> I therefore told the bishop that we considered ourselves called of God to labor principally among the German population, and that thus far our labor had not been in vain. To this he replied that the German language could not exist much longer in this country, etc. I rejoined, that if this should ever be the case, it would then be time enough to discontinue preaching in German, and gave as my opinion that this would not very soon occur, but that the German language would rather increase, at least as the immigration from the old world would continue. I then gave him my views, in which I expected my brethren to concur, and made him the following offer: "If you will give us German circuits, districts and conferences, we are willing to make your

church ours, be one people with you, and have one and the same church government." "This cannot be - it would not be expedient," was the bishop's reply.[10]

It should be understood that this was a very amicable discussion, as their relationship and the broader one between the two groups continued to be cordial. Asbury certainly could not have foreseen the mid-nineteenth century influx of German immigration, and later he and other Methodist leaders encouraged work among the Germans in their own language.

Meanwhile the "So-Called Albright People" continued to move toward becoming a distinct religious organization. The name "Evangelical Association" ("Evangelische Gemeinschaft" in German, in which Gemeinschaft could also be translated as "fellowship" or "community") was taken in 1816, and would be used until 1922 when it became "The Evangelical Church."

The Evangelische Gemeinschaft truly was a community or fellowship of believers, as well as an association. Belief in a personal experience of salvation was of the utmost importance to Evangelicals, and like the United Brethren, development into a separate denomination with an episcopal form of organization was somewhat haphazard and took years to develop. As J.W. Krecker states:

> It is interesting and significant that Evangelical United Brethrenism, from the beginnings of either branch, laid accent upon voluntary fellowship in evangelistic service, not ecclesiastical machinery; though necessarily, organization and discipline and machinery had to come.[11]

9

As the Evangelical Association began to grow and to expand into new areas, there was some increase in English-speaking ministers. However, this was short-lived, and by the early 1830s, little work in English was being carried out by Evangelicals. John Seybert, who became a very influential Evangelical bishop, was a leader of the pro-German forces, stating in 1835:

> The English speaking people were already amply provided for in this particular, by other churches. The Germans are in special need. Our church should work among them, and for their benefit. If the Evangelical Association does not help the Germans in the United States, nobody else will. God has commissioned the ministry of the Evangelical Association for the very purpose of bringing the Gospel with its light and life to the neglected German population of this country.[12]

By 1843, the Evangelical Association had again moved away from this "German first" stance, and was beginning to accept the use of English where it could promote Evangelical growth. Clearly, the trend in the eastern states was toward more rather than less use of English, particularly among the young people, and some work in English was finally encouraged.[13]

It was not long, however, before another major event began to unfold, which would again rekindle the use of German. This was the expansion in the late 1840s of German immigration, which would continue throughout the second half of the nineteenth century. Some of these German immigrants settled in eastern states such as Pennsylvania and Maryland, while others moved into Ohio, Illinois and Indiana. Wisconsin, Iowa and then Minnesota would be the western frontier of the 1840s and 1850s, and many German immigrants who sought land of their own went to these areas.

The Evangelical Association, which had committed to a ministry to the German-speaking along with some accommodation to English, did not shrink from its new challenge. Instead, it sought to meet the challenge and to send German-speaking Evangelical ministers to the new areas of German settlement. The next chapter will elaborate on this, as the Evangelische Gemeinschaft moves into Minnesota.

Methodists and United Brethren also moved westward and into Minnesota by the 1850s, and a short summary of their early work in Minnesota is given below. Since this is a study of the Evangelicals, however, the United Brethren and Methodists are not part of the discussion again until the 1940s when Evangelicals and United Brethren joined to form the Evangelical United Brethren Church, and then in the 1960s when the E.U.B.'s merged with the Methodists into the United Methodist Church.

Methodism moved westward into primarily English-speaking settlements, but also now responded to the new influx of immigrants who did not speak English. Both German and Scandinavian missions and then districts within Methodist Conferences were established. John Plank was the first German Methodist minister to go into Minnesota, in 1850. Others followed, and German Methodism continued in Minnesota until German Methodists joined the Minnesota Conference (Methodist Episcopal) in 1924.[14]

The United Brethren also sent ministers into the new areas of settlement, and since the change from German to English had already been made by mid-century, their mission was to English-speaking settlers. The first United Brethren minister in Minnesota was Edmund Clow, who arrived in 1854. He was followed by others, and while many United Brethren appointments were established, maintaining them all proved difficult. The United Brethren thus remained small and overwhelmingly rural in Minnesota throughout the nineteenth century.[15]

Notes

[1] Paul Himmel Eller, *These Evangelical United Brethren* (Dayton, 1957), p. 17.

[2] K. James Stein, in Herman B. Teeter, "Our Common Frontier Heritage," *Together* (May 1968), p. 22.

[3] Eller, *These E.U.B.s* p. 23.

[4] *Ibid.,* p. 41.

[5] Thelma Ballinger Boeder, "Wending One's Way Through Methodism – The History and the Records," *Minnesota Genealogist,* (Vol.24, No.2) p. 52.

[6] Maldwyn L. Edwards, "John Wesley," Nolan B. Harmon, ed., *Encyclopedia of World Methodism* (Nashville, 1974), p. 2497.

7 Boeder, "Wending One's Way Through Methodism," *Minnesota Genealogist*, p. 52.

8 Paul W. Milhouse, "Early Associations of Evangelical United Brethren and Methodists," *The Telescope Messenger*, Vol. 129, No. 23 (Nov.9, 1963), p. 5.

9 Eller, *These E.U.B.s*, p. 46.

10 Dreisbach's Journal, quoted in W.W. Orwig, *History of the Evangelical Association*, p. 57, in Raymond W. Albright, *A History of the Evangelical Church*, (Harrisburg, 1942) pp. 68-69.

11 Joe Willard Krecker, "On the 40th Anniversary of a Church Union," *The Telescope Messenger*, Vol. 128, No.20 (Sept. 29, 1962), p. 27.

12 S.P. Spreng, *Life of Seybert*, p. 151, in Albright, *A History of the Evangelical Church*, pp. 238-239.

13 It should be noted that the United Brethren made more and earlier accommodations to the English language while still maintaining a German-speaking ministry as well. The transition to English was virtually complete by the mid-nineteenth century.

14 T. Otto Nall, *Forever Beginning: A History of the United Methodist Church and Her Antecedents in Minnesota to 1969* (Nashville, 1973), pp. 54-60.

15 Richard A. Gist, "The 'Failures' of the Church of the United Brethren in Christ in Minnesota," in *Reports and Proceedings of the 1970 Assembly of the Commission on Archives and History in the North Central Jurisdiction of the United Methodist Church, meeting at Hamline University*, St. Paul, Minnesota, July 7-9, 1970.

Chapter Two

Moving Into Minnesota: 1850 – 1867

Germans Immigrate into Wisconsin and Minnesota

By the 1830s and 1840s German immigrants were arriving in the United States in ever-increasing numbers. Some settled in eastern cities, but many chose to move westward to acquire land. Land in the Midwest was being opened up to white settlement as the Native Americans then inhabiting the land were pushed further and further westward. Many new German immigrants joined other white settlers in Wisconsin, some of them settling in the Milwaukee area, while others went further west and north into Green Lake, Marquette and Waushara counties.

Living in German settlements in Wisconsin gave these new immigrants time to get somewhat acclimated to the new country.

15

Many of them stayed in Wisconsin, while others after some months or even years, prepared to move further west. Minnesota Territory was the frontier at that time, and must have seemed very daunting to these recent arrivals, most of whom spoke little or no English when they arrived in this country. The westward lure was more and cheaper land, particularly after the 1851 Treaty of Traverse des Sioux in which the Dakota Native Americans gave up all of their land in Minnesota except for two reservations each twenty miles wide and about seventy miles long bordering the upper Minnesota River.[1]

While Wisconsin was also still pretty much frontier country, the new Minnesota Territory was even more sparsely settled. Settlers moved west from Wisconsin in covered wagons drawn by oxen, or horses if they could afford them. There were no trains or other more convenient forms of transportation available until later. They found few white settlements of any size; St. Paul was the largest town, and had a population of 1,112 in 1850.[2] Once these new settlers bought land, they had to clear it (no easy task), plant crops, build a cabin and some shelter for their animals, all the while keeping an eye out for Native Americans who for the most part they feared and disdained. While the land was fertile, crops did not grow themselves, and the climate could be harsh and unforgiving. Weeks and often months of toil might result in little or nothing to show for it.

Isolation was also an issue for many settlers, particularly the women; some could adjust and some could not. Even though family groups or neighbors from the same part of Germany often settled near each other, loneliness and self-sufficiency were part and parcel of pioneer life. Sickness, injury and death of the young were all too common, as were farm accidents and early deaths of mothers in childbirth.

We can hardly imagine what it would have been like for people such as my great-grandparents Gottfried and Ottilie Oesterle who came from Germany to the United States in 1859. They spent a year and a half in Waushara County, Wisconsin, and then moved into Minnesota and settled near Maple Grove (about forty miles west of Minneapolis) in 1861. By 1864 they had six living children (one child died on the ship coming to the U.S. in 1859), but in November 1864 typhoid fever killed three of the children (eight-year-old Julius, four-year-old Ida, and three-year-old Gustav). Countless other settlers experienced similar tragedies, and we can really only marvel at their strength and fortitude.

The Evangelische Gemeinschaft Moves West

As German immigrants moved westward and settled on the frontier, the Evangelische Gemeinschaft was not far behind. When large numbers of Germans came into Wisconsin in the late 1840s and early 1850s, Evangelical ministers followed them and sought out the new German settlers, bringing them the gospel as they understood it. Wisconsin had been part of the Illinois Conference until 1856; in that year a separate Wisconsin Conference was established. Evangelical congregations were located in towns such as Milwaukee and Sheboygan, and in Marquette, Green Lake, and Waushara counties, where non-urban German settlements were concentrated.

In that same year of 1856 the newly-organized Wisconsin

Conference responded to a request for an Evangelical minister from two Evangelical families in Minnesota. These were the Gagstetters and Laschingers, who had joined the Evangelische Gemeinschaft in Canada. They then came to the United States and settled south of St. Paul. They had asked for a minister through the Canadian Conference, which relayed the request to the Wisconsin Conference which then responded. The first minister appointed to Minnesota was not able to take up his appointment there, so in Fall 1856 a new minister was appointed to go into Minnesota Territory. This was Andrew Tarnutzer, who first set foot on Minnesota soil in November 1856 after crossing the Mississippi River at Winona.

After several weeks in that area, he proceeded on to St. Paul, and found the Gagstetter and Laschinger families he had been told about. Here, five miles south of St. Paul, he organized the first Evangelical class in Minnesota in March 1857. He then organized a second class in the town of St. Paul a few days later. His mission was to search out and preach to German immigrants who were sometimes already Evangelicals and sometimes not.[3]

Another Evangelical minister, August Huelster, was also assigned to Minnesota in 1857. He traveled and preached in various places where there were German immigrants and Evangelical families, while Tarnutzer remained in St. Paul where the first Evangelical church (St. Paul First) was built in 1857. By the end of 1858 (the year that Minnesota became a state) there were 227 members of the Evangelische Gemeinschaft in Minnesota, and in 1859 Minnesota Evangelicals became part of the newly-formed Iowa Conference which also included all other territory west of the Mississippi River.

By 1860 there were eleven men stationed in Minnesota, serving different fields or circuits where there were some Evangelicals and other Germans who had no or different religious affiliations. Circuits covered a lot of territory. These ministers were not traveling from place to place in heated or air-conditioned comfort. A description of the trip to the Crow River field made by August Huelster in 1857 gives us a very good idea of what these early Evangelical ministers experienced:

> He found great swarms of blood-thirsty mosquitoes who tormented man and beast. Because it had previously rained considerably, the river was high, and when he crossed it, there being no bridge, he and his horse were nearly drowned. His grip was carried away by the stream, and he never recovered it again. The water was from eight to ten feet deep where he forded.[4]

While all of the travel done by these circuit-riding ministers was not this hair-raising, it was generally strenuous and extensive. Having a circuit of several widespread appointments or classes which met in peoples' homes required much travel from one appointment to the next. So, services were not necessarily held on Sundays, but on weekdays as well, depending on when the minister could reach that point on his circuit.

Most of these early ministers were young men, and with the travel and weather conditions that they faced, it behooved them to be strong and healthy as well. August Huelster, however, who was the second Evangelical minister to go into Minnesota, was very slight and weighed 100 pounds when he first began his ministry in Wisconsin at age eighteen![5]   The over-whelming majority of these early Evangelical ministers were not from the privileged class or from cities, but were generally farmers' sons who were thus used to hard physical work.

Many more settlers were coming into Minnesota by the mid and late 1850s, so the Evangelical ministers continued to seek them out, preaching to the converted and the unconverted. Many of these settlers had not had preaching services available to them for some time, often several years. So usually they welcomed a minister who could speak the mother tongue, whatever denomination he might represent. The Evangelical ministers thus were usually welcomed to an area of German settlement, and after preaching to people in a given area they then organized classes where their preaching was successful. In the late 1850s in addition to the classes formed in and near St. Paul, they established classes near Preston, East Prairie, New Trier and Maple Grove.

The Evangelische Gemeinschaft in Faribault County
Settlers, some of them German, first moved into Faribault County (see map, p. xxiii) in the mid-1850s. They settled near the Blue Earth River, where both timber and water were available. Beyond the timbered river area lay the open prairie, dotted with sloughs and prairie pot holes. Settlers, German or otherwise, contended with the usual conditions and problems of settlers elsewhere; uncertain weather conditions, illness and death, isolation, and lots of hard work. Self reliance was an absolute must for the situations faced by settlers, while at the same time they often counted on neighbors for help and reciprocated when needed.

20

There were no religious services held in the Blue Earth area (at least for Germans) until Fall 1860, when Evangelical minister J.H. Schmitt of the New Ulm Circuit heard about these German settlers and came to the area and asked if he might preach to them. Many of the German settlers were or had been at least nominally Lutherans and members of the state church in the provinces of Germany from which they came. Some of these people were receptive to the Evangelical message requiring a conversion experience, while others were not. In any case, Rev. Schmitt was able to organize a class, and in 1866 a church building was erected (Blue Earth Immanuel,[6] see map p. xxiii) four miles east of the present town of Blue Earth.

German immigrants continued to settle in Faribault County, sometimes most recently coming from Illinois or Wisconsin. They often had large families and eight to fifteen children in a family was not uncommon. As previously mentioned, the early death of infants and children, plus mothers dying in childbirth and leaving large families behind, was not uncommon either. The circuit-riding ministers and church communities that they helped to establish gave comfort and solace in times of loss and need; they were also there in more joyous times of weddings and baptisms. The Blue Earth Immanuel Church discussed above had recorded 255 baptisms by 1875, a truly astronomical figure for a less than fifteen year period.[7]

Germans were settling in other parts of Faribault County also, and a class was established near Rice Lake where Germans had first settled in 1856. Rev. Schmitt came from Blue Earth in Fall 1860 to preach at Rice Lake, and while many settlers were happy to have services in the German language, there were some in the area who opposed Rev. Schmitt's preaching. They were concerned because he was not preaching Lutheran doctrine, and agitated against him among their neighbors.[8] The Evangelische Gemeinschaft was able to gain a foothold in the area, however, and a class was organized at Rice Lake in Spring 1861 with eleven members. Services for this congregation (Rice Lake Emmanuel, see map, p. xxiii) were then held in members' homes for many years.

The Dakota Conflict of 1862

A stark reminder that much of Minnesota was still very much a frontier of white settlement came in August 1862 with the outbreak of the Dakota Conflict. As a noted scholar of that conflict states:

> Frustrated and provoked by a series of broken promises and by reservation policies that forced cultural change, Dakota Indian warriors began killing white traders and settlers in August 1862. The fighting lasted six weeks and took the lives of nearly five hundred whites, mostly civilians, and an unknown but substantial number of Indians. Twenty-three southwestern Minnesota counties were virtually depopulated.[9]

Many of the white settlers who lost their lives were German settlers, including a fair number of Evangelicals who had come to Brown, Nicollet, and Renville counties by 1860. Evangelical classes had been formed in that area, and among the white settlers

22

who lost their lives were more than seventy members of the Evangelische Gemeinschaft, including ministers Louis Seder and August Nierens.[10]

This was a sad and tragic time for the Minnesota Conference and for the State of Minnesota's native and more newly arrived inhabitants. It would be many years before the issue of the seizure of Native American land through broken treaties would begin to see the light of day; it is an issue unfortunately not yet justly resolved.

Continued Expansion and Growth in the 1860s

The Civil War was raging in the early 1860s and many Minnesotans, including recent German immigrants, fought in Minnesota regiments in the Union Army. The Evangelische Gemeinschaft had from its beginnings opposed slavery, and its membership was in all states loyal to the Union. And while the war was tragically divisive for the country as a whole, it in some ways helped German and other immigrants who fought for and supported the Union cause to feel more like they now belonged in their new country.

In the late 1860s, after the Civil War had ended, the Evangelische Gemeinschaft continued to expand into different areas in Minnesota. Usually they went where they heard that German or more particularly German Evangelicals, had settled. Among the new classes formed during this time was Dunbar Zion, (see map p. xxiii) again in Faribault County, near Rice Lake. Several families had come to Dunbar township from Wisconsin in 1865; Christoph Brill of the Evangelische Gemeinschaft found them and received permission to preach to them. They were converted at an Evangelical camp meeting at Blue Earth in the Summer of 1866 and this new class then became part of the Blue Earth Circuit.

The camp meeting was a very important and integral part of the work of the Evangelische Gemeinschaft. These camp meetings were in the early days generally held in a settler's grove; they were thus sometimes called "bush" or "grove" meetings, and were basically revival meetings. People would attend from miles around, mostly those sincere in intention but some out of curiosity or scorn.

Some of these camp meetings lasted for days, with the people and ministers camped on the grounds and returning home to attend to chores and then returning to the camp meeting. These protracted camp meetings were often the place where people felt convicted of their own sinfulness by the minister's exhortations, and were brought to their knees in the conversion experience which the Evangelische Gemeinschaft felt was the cornerstone of becoming a genuine Christian. Those who preached at or attended them usually described them as filled with emotionally verbal demonstrations of the Spirit.

The camp meetings through these early years served a major function and were a focal point for the spreading of the gospel as the Evangelische Gemeinschaft understood it. However, all of the services of the Gemeinschaft were not of this nature. On the contrary, regular weekly worship services on Sunday (or whenever they could be held in those days) were fairly formal and reflected a sense of reverence and piety. This can be seen very clearly in the hymns in the Evangelische Gesangbuch (Evangelical songbook/hymnal). These early Evangelicals were able to combine many modes of expression in their worship and/or evangelistic services.

As stated earlier in this chapter, the Evangelische Gemeinschaft first sent ministers into Minnesota from the Wisconsin Conference in 1856. Within two years (by the end of 1858) the Gemeinschaft numbered 227 in Minnesota, 123 of whom were new members that year.[11] Just two years later and after Minnesota had been placed under the jurisdiction of the Iowa Conference, there were 430 members. Even with the loss of Evangelical lives in the Dakota Conflict of 1862, membership was up to 784 by 1863.

New missions were established in promising areas, and new appointments added to established circuits where more Germans were coming into the area involved. Very often classes or appointments were formed where there were one or two Evangelical families with adequate leadership to keep the class functioning in the minister's absence while tending to the rest of his circuit. These classes were often called by these families' names until an actual church structure was built, since the classes met in family homes, often for years, before constructing a church building. Churches were built with the labor of building usually by the church members themselves, on land often donated by one of the founding families.

By 1867 – the last year that Minnesota was part of the Iowa Conference – there were 1,585 members of the Evangelische Gemeinschaft in Minnesota, served by eighteen ministers. This was the work of less than twelve years. A time of even greater growth was just ahead for the Minnesota Conference in the next quarter-century.

Notes

1 Kenneth Carley, *The Sioux Uprising of 1862* (St. Paul, 1976), p.3.

2 U.S. Department of Commerce, Bureau of the Census, *Seventh Census of the United States, 1850: Population.*

3 Albert H. Utzinger, *History of the Minnesota Conference of the Evangelical Association: 1856 to 1922* (Cleveland, 1922), pp. 15-16.

4 *Ibid.*, p. 19

5 August Huelster, *Miracle of Grace,* English translation of *Gnadenwunder,* (Cleveland, 1908) p. 90.

6 Re: *I*mmanuel/*E*mmanuel – spelling with an "I" or an "E" varies with time and place. The phrase from the hymn "Marching to Zion" from which this book's title is taken uses "I," i.e., "Marching Through *I*mmanuel's Ground." Blue Earth *I*mmanuel also uses "I," while other churches in the study used "*E*mmanuel." Some churches used both "I" and "E" at different times; I have selected the one they seemed to use most consistently.

7 Blue Earth Immanuel, *Kirchen Buch: Taufen* (Church Record Book, Baptisms) 1860-1875.

8 Utzinger, *History of the Minnesota Conference*, p. 430.

9 Gary Clayton Anderson and Alan R. Woolworth, eds., *Through Dakota Eyes* (St. Paul, 1988), p. 1.

10 Utzinger, *History of the Minnesota Conference*, p. 29

11 Membership figures in this chapter are all taken from Utzinger, *History of the Minnesota Conference.*

Chapter Three

A Growing Church: 1868 – 1890

Post-Civil War America/Minnesota

In many ways, the United States was a country of regional contrasts in the years following the Civil War. The Northeast, with its many large cities, saw continued growth in industry and commerce. The South having so recently lost the Civil War was in chaos and facing a long and arduous rebuilding process. Some of the easternmost mid-western states (Ohio, Michigan), were quite settled and becoming more industrialized, with the central mid-western states not far behind. The more western states of the Midwest were, however, still the frontier, since the "real west" was only sparsely settled by whites and was for the most part still inhabited by Native Americans.

Minnesota was still very much a frontier state in the late

1860s, with the southeastern portion the most settled. The northern part of the state was still largely inhabited by Ojibway (Chippewa) Indians, with their lands being obtained and logged by white settlers coming later. The western part of the state, particularly the southwestern portion, was ripe for white settlement since the Dakota (Sioux) Indians had been forcibly moved west after the Dakota Conflict of 1862. Also the Homestead Act had been passed in 1862, whereby a person (U.S. citizens and non-citizens) could stake out a claim to 160 acres, build a "dwelling" on it, make some "improvements" within a five-year period, and then claim title to the land.

During and particularly after the Civil War, people from more settled eastern states began moving into areas in south central and southwestern Minnesota. Many European immigrants had spent some time in more eastern states and/or in neighboring Wisconsin, while many others headed directly to Minnesota from their country of origin. The majority of these immigrants were coming from Germany and Norway, with a smattering of other nationalities as well.

The religious affiliations of these new settlers in south central and southwestern Minnesota followed them. Those who often came first from the eastern states and tended to settle in the villages were of English descent. They generally were Episcopalian, Congregationalists, or Methodists, and founded their churches most often in town and occasionally in the country. Some new settlers were German Roman Catholics who founded parishes where there was enough support to do so. However, the majority of Germans coming to Minnesota were from northern Germany and thus Lutheran, as were the

Norwegians. Both German and Norwegian Lutheran churches were formed, with services conducted in German or Norwegian.

In addition to these major denominations/religious groups, there were some German Evangelicals who also settled in these areas. As was discussed in the last chapter, the Evangelical Association (Evangelische Gemeinschaft) sent ministers into Minnesota to serve these Evangelicals and to preach the gospel to other Germans as well.

Formation of the Minnesota Conference

With the growth of the Evangelische Gemeinschaft in Minnesota during the 1850s and 1860s resulting in 1,585 members by 1867,[1] the Minnesota churches were detached from the Iowa Conference and became a separate Minnesota Conference. Arrangements were made for this at the 1867 Iowa Conference session, and the newly formed Minnesota Conference first met in April 1868 at Emmanuel's Church, Cannon Circuit (later Farmington).

The new conference continued to work in all areas with already established congregations, or more accurately "classes," with class leaders who conducted services in the circuit-riding ministers' absences. These class leaders were generally lay members who had some education and leadership skills. Several classes in the same general vicinity would then make up one charge or appointment. The Gemeinschaft also moved into areas of new settlement in Minnesota and concentrated on areas where there were some Evangelicals and where there was new German settlement further west of already settled areas.

Evangelical Growth in Faribault County

As was noted in the last chapter, the Evangelische Gemeinschaft moved into Faribault County in 1860. One church had been built by 1868 (Blue Earth Immanuel), and there were other preaching appointments scattered around the county in areas of German settlement. The major appointments were those at Rice Lake and Dunbar, both discussed in the last chapter. All of these appointments and churches were part of the Blue Earth Circuit in these early years, with Blue Earth Immanuel being the largest church in the Minnesota Conference for many years in the nineteenth century.

Blue Earth Immanuel was, as was true for many churches in areas of new settlement, the religious and social center of the surrounding rural community. Immanuel provided worship services, Sunday School, prayer meetings, and periodic revival and evangelistic services and camp meetings. Joy was experienced in weddings, baptisms, and social gatherings such as ice cream socials and picnics. The church was also the source of strength and comfort to its people in times of crisis, sickness, and death. It helped solidify and strengthen families and neighbors with the bonds of a common faith and language. All services were in German, records were kept in German, and children in Sunday School were taught German as an integral part of their lessons. Immanuel built a new, larger building in 1887, and remained the largest country church in the Conference for many years.[2]

The other Blue Earth church, Salem, (see map p. xxiii) was an outgrowth of rural Immanuel and was one of the first Evangelical churches to be located in a town in a primarily rural

30

area. Area farmers often moved to town when they retired from farming, generally leaving the farm to a son. The ministers from Immanuel first served these Evangelical townspeople, and a church building was erected in Blue Earth in 1881. The Blue Earth City Mission was formed in 1887 and from 1888 on, Salem and Immanuel were separate appointments each served by their own ministers.

The other classes or appointments in Faribault County were part of the Wells Circuit after 1873. The Rice Lake and Dunbar classes had been organized in the early 1860s. A church was built in Dunbar Township in 1874, Dunbar Zion. In 1891 the church building was moved two miles in order to be closer to where members lived. Apparently this seemingly short move was felt to be worthwhile, since poor roads and slow transportation by horse and buggy made two miles seem much further than it would seem now.

The Rice Lake class continued to meet in members' homes until 1880 when they built Emmanuel's Church on the shore of Rice Lake. Its ninetieth anniversary booklet states: "In it sinners were converted, believers grew in grace, and God's work prospered."[3] There was also a class in Brush Creek Township (a few miles southwest of Rice Lake, see map p. xxiii) and this class built Tabor Church in 1886. This church was also called "the windmill" because of a large windmill located near the church which was visible for quite a distance. Churches having two names were not unusual. There would always be an "official" name such as "Zion" or "Salem," and then perhaps another name such as "the windmill" which related to a prominent feature in the landscape.

The last Evangelical church to be organized in Faribault County was Wells Salem (see map p. xxiii). This was a "town" church, and like Blue Earth Salem, it had its roots in the country. Retired older farmers from primarily Dunbar but also Rice Lake and Brush Creek, started to move into Wells. They, along with other non-Lutheran Germans, formed the nucleus of Wells Salem. Services were first held in Wells in the early 1880s, and the congregation was organized in 1887. In 1888, they used a tiny chapel which had an inscription over the door saying, "Die Salem's Kapelle der Evangelische Gemeinschaft" (The Salem's Chapel of the Evangelical Association), and the distinction of having the smallest church building in the Minnesota Conference until a much larger church was built in 1892.[4]

All of the churches in Faribault County were within thirty miles of each other. The four churches on the Wells circuit had no more than seven miles separating one from the next. The families that made up these churches were for the most part interrelated; church records verify these familial ties.

These inter-relationships are very clearly illustrated by information gathered in an interview with two sisters who had been members of the Brush Creek church. They indicated that their father's sister was the wife of a man named Henry Miller, another of their father's sisters married Miller's brother William, and their mother's sister married the other Miller brother, Fred.[5]

These kinds of inter-relationships were not at all unusual. Generally the German immigrants who settled in a certain area came from the same provinces in Germany; many of those in Faribault County were from the provinces of Posen or Pomerania, where the state church was Protestant/Lutheran. Those who became members of the Evangelishe Gemeinschaft, along with those of other religious affiliations, tended to marry within their own groups. These family ties helped to strengthen ties of culture and heritage as well. Maintaining the German language in the church and at home was very important to the immigrants, while at the same time many of them (particularly the men and children) learned to speak English as soon as possible. The children were more likely to learn to read and write English as well, once there was some form of public education in the area.

Beginnings of the Evangelische Gemeinschaft in Southwestern Minnesota

As the Evangelische Gemeinschaft followed German immigrants into different parts of Minnesota, they attempted to establish footholds in areas both where there were many Germans and where German settlers were less numerous. The earlier discussion of Evangelicals in Faribault County showed six Evangelical classes/congregations within thirty miles; those in southwest Minnesota were much more widely scattered.

The ten Evangelical churches in southwest Minnesota were located in six different counties; they ranged from just west of Blue Earth at Fairmont, to the southwest corner of the state at Luverne, up to Hendricks on the western (South Dakota) border and then southeast to Marshall. (see map p. xxiii).

The white settlement of southwest Minnesota was delayed by the Dakota Conflict of 1862, as few settlers moved into the area until after most of the Dakota were forcibly moved west into

33

Dakota Territory. When immigration into this area did increase after the Civil War, no one ethnic group dominated. There were native-born Americans of primarily English background, and Swedes, Norwegians, Germans, and later Belgians, Dutch, Icelandic and Polish immigrants. Each ethnic group settled together in the country and sometimes in villages as well, although there were (and are) even some towns dominated by one ethnic group. Thus, there was a distinct "patchwork quilt" effect, with each nationality representing one or more squares of the quilt. Certainly other areas contained a diversity of groups as well, but southwest Minnesota was probably the most diverse of the areas where the Evangelische Gemeinschaft founded early churches.

The first minister of the Evangelische Gemeinschaft to preach in southwest Minnesota was Reverend Peter Bott. He was stationed on the Blue Earth circuit with the Reverend E. J. Hielscher and starting in 1870 he circuit-rode west of Blue Earth setting up new Evangelical classes wherever possible. One of the first of these classes was called Elm Creek (near Welcome) where Germans coming from Preston, Minnesota had settled. More German settlers arrived from Wisconsin, and an Evangelical class was organized in 1871. The services were held in members' homes until 1891 when Welcome Emmanuel Church (see map p. xxiii) was completed with most of the work being done by members. The eighty-fifth anniversary booklet for Emmanuel Evangelical United Brethren Church states that $1,394.74 was collected to pay for the building, leaving a balance of $33.95. As this history's authors state, "Leave it to the Pioneers! They surely did get things done."[6]

The Elm Creek/Welcome appointment was one of many in the Fairmont/Jackson area of Martin County. Some grew and prospered, while others shriveled and died. With appointments covering large areas with many miles to travel, it was incumbent upon the minister to be a capable handler of horses as well as a saver of souls. For example, the historical account from Welcome points out that Reverend W. A. Juedes who was stationed there in 1889, was a big, strong man, an excellent driver of horses, and a very powerful preacher.[7]

Fairmont was not far from Welcome, and in 1890 Evangelical ministers helped organize a class there. This class built a church, Fairmont Salem, (see map p. xxiii) in 1900. Fairmont Salem and Welcome Emmanuel were historically served by the same minister. The Reverend Peter Bott, the first Evangelical minister in Martin County, must have also been a good horseman as well as an effective minister, as he is mentioned as the first Evangelical minister in many areas of southwestern Minnesota.

One of these areas was near Luverne in Rock County on the Dakota Territory border, where he arrived in 1872. Permanent white settlement had begun in the area in 1867, with some German settlers arriving in 1871. These were the people Reverend Bott sought out, and a class was organized in 1874. After meeting in homes for a while they built a temporary meeting place of boards, horse blankets and bed sheets.[8] Also in 1874 they officially became the Ebenezer Church of the Evangelische Gemeinschaft (see map p. xxiii) and made plans to construct a building that year on six acres they had purchased from the railroad. However, the plans were put on hold when grasshoppers destroyed the crop. The building was erected in 1875, and Utzinger says:

> Probably no church in our Conference was erected for use in so short a time. The lumber for the building was brought to the place on Wednesday, July 7th and on Friday evening, the 9th, the first service was held in it.[9]

In reflecting on the building at Pleasant View Ebenezer, and of so many Evangelical and other pioneer churches, one is impressed by the pioneers' tenacity and devotion. While there were certainly times of happiness and joy, there were also many catastrophes and crises to confront. An account of the early years of Pleasant View Ebenezer refers to the grasshopper plague which hit the area in the mid-1870s, and to the typhoid epidemic during the same years. This account also describes how Pleasant View Evangelical minister Balthazar Simon and his wife nursed the sick for seven weeks.[10]

Other accounts of the same time period in other areas refer to blizzards, cyclones, heavy rains, high water, mud and prairie fires, as well as to epidemics of diphtheria, small pox and scarlet fever, which resulted in many deaths of the young as well as the old. That these early Evangelicals (and those of other persuasions as well) took the time and had the energy to build and sustain churches in the face of such trials and tribulations is nothing short of amazing. These trials and tribulations certainly gave these pioneers the opportunity to bear visible witness to their faith.

One of Luverne Ebenezer's ministers, C. W. Wolthausen,

began Evangelical services in the nearby village of Steen in 1894. A congregation was then organized in Steen, and a church built that same year, 1894. This church, Steen Salem (see map p. xxiii) was then served by Luverne ministers in a two-charge appointment.

One of the first "town" churches of the Evangelische Gemeinschaft to be established in southwest Minnesota was Worthington Emmanuel (see map p. xxiii). A number of Evangelical families along with many others were brought west from Illinois by land agents. Many of them had come originally from East Friesland, a province in the northwestern part of Germany bordering on Holland.

This was in the mid-1870s, and Evangelical minister Balthazar Simon first preached to Evangelicals in Worthington in 1877. Services were conducted in homes, halls and established churches for a number of years, until 1891 when the congregation built their first church building. There were a few small country appointments near Worthington, and the small Bethel Evangelical Church (ten miles southeast of Worthington) was served by Worthington ministers for many years.

As was discussed earlier, the Evangelical churches in southwestern Minnesota were not clustered as closely together as in Faribault County. They were founded in areas of German settlement, and German settlement was not that large in southwest Minnesota. Consequently, Evangelical circuit-riders had to travel great distances from one preaching point to another, and it was not easy to adequately maintain the more scattered or isolated ones. Considering the difficulties involved, it is remarkable that a number of Evangelical churches did succeed in spite of these difficulties.

The Hendricks Zion, or "New Grove," Church (see map p. xxiii) was one such church. The name "New Grove," is described as follows:

> In the 1870s the United States government required that purchasers of land in this area must make improvements with the intent of permanent residence instead of holding it for speculation. A stipulation was the planting of trees; hence the term "tree claim." Tradition says a massive prairie fire swept the area, devastating the trees and numerous new groves were planted to replace them. Hence, the area became known for its many new emerging groves as a landmark for pioneer travelers and the term "new grove," became a permanent name.[11]

Some Evangelical families had settled south of what is now the town of Hendricks in the mid-1870s, and shortly thereafter Reverend F. R. Plantikow visited these settlers and preached to them in their homes. Julius Fandrey is shown as both one of the founding members and as the third minister of the New Grove congregation, and the church history notes that he purchased land in the New Grove area and then sold parcels to Evangelicals in the area.[12] This practice, or variations of it, took place in some other areas of Evangelical settlement as well. In any case, the New Grove Church building was constructed in 1884, and was about six miles from the town of Hendricks.

Two other Evangelical churches were organized on the far southwestern Minnesota border, in Pipestone County. The first white settlers arrived in the area around 1874. Evangelical minister Ludwig Passer first came from the Luverne mission to preach to the Germans in the Pipestone area in 1879. As was customary, these early converts met in each others' homes for several years. They organized a congregation, Pipestone Salem, in 1886 and built a small church in 1887 (see map p. xxiii). This building soon became too small, and a larger church was built in 1899, which still serves this congregation one hundred years later.

The Pipestone "town" church had its origins in meetings at Roe's Trading Post, starting in the late 1880s. A church, Pipestone Zion, (see map p. xxiii) was built in 1898 in what were then the outskirts of the town, and this church and Pipestone Salem were historically served by the same minister.

The remaining two Evangelical churches in southwest Minnesota are those at Marshall and Clifton. Reverend H. Loewen of the Dakota Conference first preached in Marshall in 1887. A congregation was organized soon after which became part of the Minnesota Conference. A church was built in the town of Marshall in 1900, and was named Salem (see map p. xxiii). This church did not have primarily rural roots, as was also true of some of the other Evangelical churches in southwest Minnesota such as Fairmont Salem, Worthington Emmanuel, and Pipestone Zion. Thus, ties with any nearby rural Evangelical churches were probably not as strong, even when the two churches involved were historically served by the same minister. For these churches there were not the multitudes of family inter-relationships between town and country church members. There were, however, large extended and inter-related family groups within particular churches in southwest Minnesota. This was particularly true in the rural churches, such as Welcome Emmanuel, Luverne Ebenezer, Hendricks Zion, and Pipestone Salem.

The Clifton Bethel Church (see map p. xxiii), a rural church served with the Salem "town" church in Marshall, was different in origin from all of the churches discussed above. This church, seven miles from Marshall, actually had its beginnings in the late 1870s in a "Union Sunday School" which was non-denominational and included people of different ethnic backgrounds. A Presbyterian church grew out of this Union Sunday School, as did Clifton Bethel of the Evangelical Association. This congregation was organized in 1894, and put up a building in 1905. Of all the churches in the three areas researched, this was the only Evangelical church whose records were never kept in German but were always in English.

This was a portent of things to come with regard to the German versus English issue. It also clearly illustrates the ethnic diversity in many parts of southwest Minnesota. This is not to say that the different ethnic groups in this area (English, German, Norwegian, Icelandic, Belgian, Dutch) all jumped into the "melting pot" when they arrived in southwest Minnesota. Each ethnic group was still likely to "stick together" geographically, in marriage, and in most other relationships. What it does say is that since there were a variety of ethnic groups living in the area, they did not stay totally isolated from each other, and were occasionally willing to cross ethnic boundaries in a united effort such as the Clifton Union Sunday School.

40

The Evangelische Gemeinschaft in Western Minnesota

The Evangelische Gemeinschaft was busy working in other parts of Minnesota as well during the last three decades of the nineteenth century. Many immigrants (primarily Scandinavians and Germans) were coming into Minnesota in search of land and a better life for themselves and their children. German immigrants, whether they came directly from Germany or from more settled parts of the United States, followed the general pattern of settling where there were other Germans. They often went to where others from the same province, or even the same village in Germany had gone to earlier. These were the people the circuit-riding ministers of the Evangelische Gemeinschaft continued to search out. As the German immigrants moved westward in Minnesota, so did the church.

By the 1870s many Norwegian and German immigrants were going into western Minnesota and on into Dakota Territory, after the Native Americans had been forced westward onto reservations. This area was part of the vast tallgrass prairie, and also contained many sloughs and wetlands. It was quite similar to the area in southwest Minnesota discussed above, although there were more trees in the river valleys.

Some German along with Norwegian immigrants had moved into the Minnesota River Valley, and also near the Yellowbank River in what is now Lac Qui Parle County (see map, p.xxiii). This was in 1870. Two Evangelical families had settled there, and in Spring 1871, Reverend A. C. Schmidt came from the Redwood Circuit to preach to them. Later that year, Reverend Schmidt "...penetrated into Dakota, but found nothing but a boundless

41

prairie."[13] What a sight that must have been, for him and many others, to see that vast and beautiful prairie stretching out to the horizon!

Over the next few years, several more Evangelical families moved into the Yellowbank area, and a congregation, Yellowbank Emmanuel, was organized in 1876 (see map p. xxiii). The first church building went up in 1878-1879 but this sanctuary soon proved too small to hold the ever-growing congregation. A larger church was built in 1881.

Revival, or camp meetings, were held in the Yellowbank area starting in 1880. In the early years, camp meetings were held in church members' groves. More permanent camp meeting grounds were then established on the banks of the Yellowbank River, just down the hill from the church and next to the parsonage. The camp meetings at Yellowbank grew and prospered, and people came from miles around to attend. The meetings would last about ten days; the women and children would often stay in tents on the campgrounds, while the men would make trips home to tend to the animals and chores.

It should also be noted that it was in the Yellowbank Emmanuel Church that the Dakota Conference was formed in 1883. Just as the Minnesota Conference had split off from the Iowa Conference in 1868, so now the Dakota Conference became independent. While this was a sign of growth and success for the Evangelische Gemeinschaft, it also meant that several of the ministers of the Minnesota Conference would now be working only in the Dakotas. With travel by horseback only, it was unlikely these two groups would continue to see each other often, if at all.

Utzinger describes their parting as follows:

> Then the conference formed a circle and bade each other a
> hearty farewell, at which many tears flowed, for some real-
> ized that it was the last time that some of them would see
> each other here below. [14]

Two other Evangelical churches in Lac Qui Parle County are very closely connected with Yellowbank Emmanuel. These are Salem and Bellingham Zion, and they were located closely togeth-er, as was true of the Evangelical churches in Faribault County. The Salem Church (see map p. xxiii) was out in open country just like Emmanuel. Salem's first church building was not a "new" building; the congregation bought the old Hay Creek Evangelical Church. They had the building dismantled, shipped by train and re-erected at the Salem site in 1883. This building burned down ten years later and a larger church was built on the site in 1893.

The Bellingham Zion Church (see map p. xxiii) grew out of the Salem Church, its members first attending services at Salem and then having services in homes and in the school. The Bellingham village school was a busy place on Sunday as the Bellingham Zion centennial history states that:

> For a period of time, three services were held in the school
> house each Sunday, one in English by the Methodist
> Episcopals (which closed in 1915), one in Norwegian by the
> Lutherans and one in German by the Evangelicals. [15]

The Evangelical congregation was organized in 1889, and Utzinger describes their building a church as follows:

In 1890 these few members began to build a church. They had the foundation nearly finished when behold, a hailstorm destroyed the crops, and they had to cease building. The next year, the Lord gave them a harvest and their church was completed. [16]

The geographical closeness of these three churches, Yellowbank Emmanuel, Salem, and Bellingham Zion, (each about four miles from one of the other two), is a reminder that transportation was slow and tedious in the nineteenth century. People traveled by foot, horseback, or horse team and buggy, and could not realistically be expected to travel more than a few miles to church, school or to shop or trade in the nearest village or town. Thus when there were a good number of German Evangelicals (or other groups) in an area, it made sense to establish a number of more easily accessible smaller churches than one large one whose radius could extend only so far. No wonder these little churches then served as focal points for their surrounding communities.

The remaining two Evangelical churches in this part of Minnesota are Fairfield Zion and Madison Ebenezer. There were some German immigrants who had settled north of Appleton in Swift County in the mid 1870s. Evangelical minister, E. J. Hilscher helped them organize a congregation, Fairfield Zion, (see map p. xxiii) in 1874 and in 1881 they bought and moved the little Yellowbank church which that congregation had outgrown. It was apparently not at all uncommon for outgrown church buildings to be sold, dismantled, and moved by rail to another location. A new larger Fairfield Zion church was built in 1895, and a barn for stabling horses while their owners were in church was built in 1896. Each family in the church was assigned one stall for their horses, and was expected to contribute ten dollars toward the building costs of the barn.[17] Nearly every rural church, and some of the town churches as well, built such stables. Services in those days tended to run quite long, and the horses needed shelter from the elements, be it snow and cold in winter or rain and heat in summer.

The Madison Ebenezer Church, known at first as the Hamlin Church because it was in Hamlin Township, had its beginnings in 1879 (see map p. xxiii). The congregation built a church in 1889 four miles south of the town of Madison, which was actually settled by more Norwegians than Germans. There were some other appointments served by Evangelical ministers in this part of western Minnesota, but for various reasons they did not prosper.

Summary

The last three decades of the nineteenth century were very busy and productive ones for the Evangelische Gemeinschaft in Minnesota. Their mission – to reach out and preach the gospel to German immigrants in their own language – was being realized on the Minnesota prairie. German language and traditions remained strong, and rural churches predominated over town churches. The Germans who had come to this part of Minnesota had come primarily to own their own land, and the church had followed them and organized congregations where there were

45

enough German Evangelicals to do so. The members of these churches were usually inter-related, which contributed to their cohesiveness and strength as a community institution.

The winds of change were blowing, however, and the next chapter will discuss the major conflicts and changes confronting the Evangelische Gemeinschaft toward the end of the nineteenth century and accelerating in the early part of the twentieth century. First, the church would be split by a conflict in its own ranks. Second, the impending issue of German versus English language usage loomed large on the horizon and had to be resolved.

Notes

[1] Utzinger, *History of the Minnesota Conference*, p. 38.

[2] *Ibid.*, p. 342.

[3] "Historical Sketch," *Ninetieth Anniversary and Rededication of the Rice Lake Evangelical United Brethren Church, 1861-1951* (1952), p. 10.

[4] "History of Salem Evangelical Sunday School," Wells United Methodist Records.

[5] Hazel and Mildred Schroeder, Interview of June 9, 1994, near Wells, Minnesota.

6 "A Brief History of the Emmanuel Evangelical United Brethren Congregation, Fox Lake Township, Martin County, Minnesota," *Eighty -fifth Anniversary of the Emmanuel Church, Evangelical United Brethren, Welcome, Minnesota, 1870-1955.*

7 *Ibid.*

8 Utzinger, *History of the Minnesota Conference,* p. 373.

9 *Ibid.,* p. 374.

10 "Former Pastors of Luverne," p. 3–4, Luverne Ebenezer records.

11 Mrs. Charles Luekens, "New Grove Zion Evangelical Church," (1969), p. 1, Hendricks Zion (New Grove) records.

12 *Ibid.*

13 Utzinger, *History of the Minnesota Conference,* p. 391.

14 *Ibid.,* p. 121. Annual Conference was held for a week in the Spring at different churches/locations within Minnesota each year. In addition to conducting Conference business, it was a time for worship, fellowship, and renewal of friendships among the ministers. The appointment of ministers to the same or a new charge/field was also made at Conference; the Bishop and Presiding Elders (later called District/Conference Superintendents) made these decisions and the ministers themselves were not involved in the decision-making until at least mid-twentieth century. Thus when the appointments were read aloud by the Bishop on Conference Sunday (with many lay people from near and far in attendance as well), it was an occasion of some suspense and excitement. This was particularly true for the ministers and their families, who might then be moving to another charge with-

in the month. In the early years, appointment to a charge was for one year; two, three, five and then seven year limits were then set by the early twentieth century, and then finally there was no set limit. Thus, particularly in earlier years the word "itinerant" was applied literally, and was not a mere figure of speech.

[15] *Zion United Methodist Church, 1889-1989*, Bellingham, Minnesota, p. 3, Bellingham Zion records. This centennial history of Bellingham Zion, which also includes information on nearby Salem and Yellowbank Emmanuel, is the most comprehensive and well-done local church history I have consulted and could be a model for any church planning to do a written history.

[16] Utzinger, *History of the Minnesota Conference*, p. 393.

[17] Swift County Historical Society, *Swift County History: A Collection of Historical Sketches and Family Histories* (Benson, Minnesota, 1979), p. 328.

Chapter Four

Politics and Language:
Division and Discord   1891 – 1921

Growth in Minnesota in the Late Nineteenth Century

The late nineteenth century saw the closing of the western frontier. The Indian wars ended with the U.S. Army's massacre of Big Foot's band of Dakotas at Wounded Knee, South Dakota in December 1890. White settlement of the West was proceeding apace, as settlers from the eastern United States and from Europe continued to move westward.

German immigration to the United States had slowed considerably by this time, although some Germans continued to arrive. Some of them came to Minnesota, where they usually found family or others from the same part of Germany. They usually went to already established communities, sometimes to cities or towns, and sometimes to rural areas where they bought land. And while the United States was still overwhelmingly rural at this time, land was not as readily available or as cheap as it had been earlier.

In Minnesota as in other places, cities, towns and rural areas were developing systems of local government, commerce and education. Community institutions like the church were a part of this growth too, as both English-speaking and ethnic churches which maintained services in their own languages were established. As mentioned earlier, churches were often focal points in their communities and held communities together.

Minnesota's Evangelicals in the Late Nineteenth Century

As we saw in the last chapter, the Evangelische Gemeinschaft established classes, congregations and churches in south central, southwestern and western Minnesota. These Evangelical churches in Minnesota were established in areas of German settlement. They reflected German culture, tradition and language, some more than others.

These churches also reflected and tried to live out the beliefs and values which the Evangelische Gemeinschaft stood for. Evangelical roots were of Wesleyan and pietistic origin (see Chapter One), and the worship services and hymns of the Evangelische Gemeinschaft reflected both devout reverence and heartfelt enthusiasm. The members of these churches tried to live their lives in accordance with their church's teachings and values. Naturally, some were more successful at this than others. Kenneth Krueger spells out these "abiding values from our pietistic heritage" as follows:

> ... a personal experience of Jesus Christ, a reverence for the Scriptures, an emphasis on godly living, a respectful attitude in church, the practice of family worship, kindness to neighbors, hospitality to strangers, courage of one's convictions, generosity in giving, reverence for elders. [1]

It must also be acknowledged that the Evangelische Gemeinschaft and some of its churches and members could sometimes be judgmental, self-righteous, narrow and parochial. Sometimes fervent belief resulted in these traits to a greater or lesser extent, and/or sometimes the personalities involved were responsible. As Krueger so succinctly notes: "The Germanic temperament can be stubborn and opinionated,"[2] and this sometimes resulted in perhaps unnecessary altercations or at least over-reaction to views other than one's own.

This could be seen at the local level where members could be, and sometimes were, expelled from the church for transgressions in word and/or deed. For example, one of my great-uncles was expelled from the Maple Grove Immanuel Church in the early years of this century when it was discovered that he had purchased a keg of beer for the French Catholic farmers participating in his barn raising.[3] People expelled from the church were sometimes lost to the Evangelical or to any church, and it is questionable whether expulsion was good for either those expelled or those doing the expelling.

The Evangelical Association
and the United Evangelical Church

Similar issues arose on the national level, most clearly shown by the split in the Evangelische Gemeinschaft in the late 1800s which resulted in two separate churches, the Evangelical Association and the United Evangelical Church. Other churches, including the United Brethren in Christ, experienced similar divisive movements and splits, so the Evangelicals were not alone in what now appears to have been a time of general ecclesiastical divisiveness.

Paul Eller states: "Between 1887 and 1891 the Evangelical Association slowly and painfully disintegrated."[4]   The major points of contention appear to have been related to the powers of bishops and the episcopal form of church governance. These issues were soon obscured by personal rivalries between two powerful bishops, J. J. Escher and Rudolph Dubs. There were charges and counter charges and bitter and costly civil suits and litigation, even though lay leadership sought an amicable settlement.   By 1894 the result was two separate churches.[5]   The Evangelical Association led by Bishop Escher retained about three-fifths of its former membership, and the remaining two-fifths formed the United Evangelical Church with Bishop Dubs.

Evangelical Association/United Evangelicals
in Minnesota

Raymond Albright calls the 1890s "...the darkest and saddest era in the history of the church."[6]   It was surely not a time to reflect on with much pride, and it was fortunate that the national division did not have a major effect in Minnesota. The real strength in the United Evangelical Church was in many of the larger conferences in eastern states such as Pennsylvania. Minnesota was in Bishop J. J. Escher's episcopal jurisdiction, and hence for the most part remained loyal to the Evangelical Association. Thus, in Minnesota local churches and families were not divided in anger and rancorous suits and counter-suits over church property as did happen elsewhere.

The United Evangelicals did, however, organize a few new congregations in western Minnesota, some of which were short-lived, and others which survived and became part of the reunited body, the Evangelical Church, in 1922. There were some United Evangelical country appointments in the Big Stone – Lac Qui Parle area, and United Evangelical appointments were also organized in the villages of Correll and Odessa, in Big Stone County just across the Minnesota River from Lac Qui Parle County with its cluster of Evangelical Association churches. The church in Odessa (Salem, see map, p.xxiii) was built in 1897, and along with the other United Evangelical churches, was part of the Des Moines United Evangelical Conference between 1897 and 1922.[7]

As noted above, the United Evangelicals and the Evangelical Association were reunited in 1922. By 1907 there was already some movement toward reconciliation, and by 1910 both groups established Commissions on Church Federation and Church Union. These commissions met jointly in 1911. In 1916 a centennial celebration of "official" Evangelical beginnings was held with both groups participating. Finally in 1922 the Evangelical Association and the United Evangelicals officially became the

Evangelical Church, a cause for much rejoicing by both clergy and lay people. While a reunited church was indeed reason for celebration, it was unfortunate that the split had occurred in the first place, diverting precious resources of time, money, intellect, and especially spirit, from the church's real mission.

The Language Issue: German Versus English

In looking at the beginnings and formation of the Evangelische Gemeinschaft in the early 1800s in Chapter One, it is clear that the German versus English language issue was one of the utmost importance. This issue continued to be important and divisive throughout the nineteenth century and well into the twentieth century. It was an issue on the national level, at the state conference level, and became an issue in almost every local congregation.

As discussed earlier, the Evangelische Gemeinschaft had sought out German-speaking immigrants and ministered to them in their own language. By the middle of the nineteenth century, however, there had been much movement toward the use of English in the church in the eastern states such as Pennsylvania. German Evangelicals in these areas were not recent immigrants, and were becoming more and more assimilated into American English-speaking culture. And by 1843 the General Conference of the Evangelische Gemeinschaft had stated that they would work with both the English and German portions of the population, while still considering their major mission to be directed toward the Germans.[8]

It was also around the middle of the nineteenth century that

German immigration to the United States started increasing. This trend continued throughout the nineteenth century, and as discussed in earlier chapters, many of the Germans wanted land and found their way to midwestern states where good farm land was still available. As we know, the Evangelische Gemeinschaft found and ministered to immigrants in Minnesota in the latter decades of the nineteenth century. These Evangelical ministers established classes and congregations in many areas, among which are those discussed in previous chapters.

The German immigrants in Minnesota, as did other immigrants in other places, kept their old country language, traditions and culture in the new homeland. German was used at home and in the church, even after immigrants had become functionally literate in English. As historian Elwyn Robinson so eloquently puts it:

> The language change was fundamental. Most immigrants became bilingual, learning English but also clinging to their native tongue. English was the language of the pocketbook and the outer shell of life without warmth; the old language, spoken at home, was the language of the most intimate and valuable experience.[9]

Thus, German remained the language of the heart and soul for Evangelicals in Minnesota for most of the nineteenth century. The children of these German immigrants learned English in school and elsewhere, but were still, for the most part, also fluent in German. Evangelical Sunday Schools played a major role in perpetuating the German language in the younger generation.

They taught the German language along with traditional Sunday School lessons, and these efforts increased as more and more children learned less and less German at home.

The language issue was debated and dealt with in different ways in different places. The 1879 General Conference Episcopal Address tried to pour oil on these troubled waters, stating:

> The most prudent discretion, and impartial procedures, are necessary to prevent friction in our congregations where both languages are spoken. Equal attention needs to be given to the rightful claims of the older – and on the other hand, to the younger... In as much as there are still differences, and will be until one language surrenders the field to the other, final adjustments are not yet possible... In all cases both languages have equal rights. Mutual patience and forbearance must be exercised. Our greatest concern is for the glory of God and the salvation of the world.[10]

It was easier said than done to resolve this emotionally charged issue in saintly or even conciliatory ways in all instances. Before the Evangelical Association/United Evangelical split in the 1890s, the German versus English issue was causing conflicts as far west as Minnesota. The Evangelical Association was more wedded to the maintenance of German in the church than were the United Evangelicals. This was especially true of the episcopal leadership of the Evangelical Association embodied in Bishop J. J. Escher, and in the more western conferences such as Minnesota which had more recent immigrants.

There was, however, some movement toward English, especially among the younger people who now spoke English as their first language. Obviously if the church was to grow, it had to keep the younger members it already had and reach out to those as yet unchurched. Reaching out only in German became less and less productive as fewer and fewer young people spoke the language well any more. For those still within the church whose first language was now English, the church often became less and less relevant.

On the other hand, those who wanted to maintain the German language (usually including older people in positions of leadership as well as many Evangelical ministers whose grasp of English was tenuous at best), were not going to go quietly away. Their battle cry was "Deutsch wir sind, und Deutsch werden wir bleiben" ("We are German and we will remain German").[11] And lest we condemn these people for being " stubborn old Germans" we need to remember why they felt as they did. While there was indeed perhaps arrogance in some of them feeling that God spoke German and German was the language of heaven, there were other factors as well. As discussed earlier, German was the language these people thought and felt in, and to preach or listen to a sermon or to sing hymns in English seemed to rob their worship of real meaning. To totally give up their language and its many layers of meaning seemed to threaten their very existence and how they defined themselves.

The Language Issue in Minnesota

German was still predominant in Minnesota Evangelical churches in the late nineteenth century. As discussed above, compromise on this issue would not come easily or quickly. This was true in Minnesota as elsewhere, and even with sincere efforts to compromise and resolve the issue amicably, it was not easy. The language dilemma is clearly illustrated by Reverend August Huelster, one of Minnesota's pioneer ministers, as he wrestled with this issue. On the one hand he gloried in and wanted to maintain the German, stating:

> ...for poetry, music, philosophy and art, the German language stands unequalled and this precious speech treasure is cast away by these parents... In order to retain this language we must use it. Who would willingly throw away a wonderful language? [12]

But then Huelster goes on to say:

> However, when circumstances confront us, we must fit ourselves into these changing conditions, and we must if there be no other way, use the English language in the preaching and in the English catechism... Thus the language question presents many problems which must be faced and met. The working out [of] these problems we must do in wisdom and much prayer. We must not abandon the German too soon; but not too late either...we have to keep the advancement and continuation of God's work in mind and if need be sacrifice over our own views and feelings. How this is to be accomplished successfully, that rests in God's hands. [13]

The language dilemma facing German Evangelicals was fundamental to other immigrant churches as well. The United Brethren had wrestled with this issue earlier in the century. In Minnesota German and Scandinavian Methodists faced the same issue, as did the German, Norwegian, Swedish and Danish Lutherans.

German to English in Southwest Minnesota

The process of change from German to English in Evangelical churches in Minnesota, as elsewhere, was hastened in areas where there were fewer Germans. Assimilation and acculturation in all areas of life were speeded up by the necessity of communicating with one's neighbors, fellow workers or schoolmates. Thus, in southwestern Minnesota, where the churches of the Evangelical Association were more scattered and not as rural, the movement toward services in English was well on its way by the early twentieth century.

Most of these churches (other than Clifton Bethel, where services had never been held in German), went through a period of transition for many years. Generally, one service a month would first be held in English, then half, and then perhaps English in the Sunday morning service and German in the evening service. Finally all services would be in English, except for an occasional German service. Catechism classes were often held in English before the language change was made in Sunday services since more and more children and young people did not read or write well enough in German to be confirmed in that language.

The switch to English was not only emotionally and spiritually traumatic for many of the older Evangelicals. Many of them, and perhaps an even higher percentage of Evangelical ministers, were not fluent speakers of English and found reading and writing the English language very difficult. For Evangelical ministers, particularly the older ones, nearly all of whom had been educated for the ministry in the German language, the switch to English was no small matter. Some of them, especially those relatively fluent in English, made the transition quite willingly. Others balked, along with older members of their congregations, and many of these latter folks only grudgingly, if at all, accepted the English. In the Welcome Emmanuel church records there is a notation for the March 26, 1919 congregational meeting stating: "Motion made and carried that the pastor is to get [an] English Bible." [14] Some older members left the Evangelical Association entirely, and affiliated with the German Lutherans who were still using the German language exclusively.

The language dilemma is well illustrated by a comment of Reverend C.G. Roesti, who in 1918 was serving the Jackson mission, an appointment near Fairmont in southwest Minnesota that later failed. He stated:

> I sincerely believe that if our good people will yield and also hold English Church mornings, there is hope for our work in Jackson. The young people and children are entitled to that, and our good old people, whom we certainly love, must surrender, if they will look well into the future of their children. [15]

The demise of this mission in the 1920s cannot be attributed solely to the language conflict, but it certainly played a part.

As for the specific Evangelical churches in southwest Minnesota, most had switched to English by the end of World War I.

A history of Nobles County published in 1908 noted that Worthington Emmanuel was already holding half of its services "in the language of the land."[16] Pipestone Zion (also a town, not country, church) completed the transition to English in 1913.[17] The other churches in this area, both town and country, had apparently made the transition to primarily English services by 1918. These were Fairmont Salem, Welcome Emmanuel, Luverne Ebenezer, Steen Salem, Pipestone Salem, Hendricks Zion, and Marshall Salem; Clifton Bethel had always conducted services in English.

World War I and the Transition to English

Clearly the transition to English had already occurred in Evangelical churches in many eastern states long before the turn of the century, and was beginning in Minnesota by this time. However, the part that World War I played in hastening this transition in Minnesota and other midwestern states cannot be overestimated. With the beginning of World War I in Europe in 1914, most American sentiment was with the Allies (England and France) and against the Axis powers (Germany and Austria). Anti-German feeling increased as the war went on, especially after the sinking of the British ship Lusitania in 1915 when 1200 American lives were lost.

This anti-Germanism developed into hysteria by the time the United States entered the war on the side of the Allies in 1917. German-Americans were increasingly subjected to harassment and abuse regardless of their political views about the war. Affirmations and demonstrations of loyalty to the United States and the Allied cause by German-Americans were often not enough to satisfy overly-zealous and often self-appointed guardians of "Americanism." The harassment and abuse of German-Americans varied by location and inclination of the non-German citizens, but was most intense in areas where there were concentrations of German-Americans and other groups in close proximity.

Anti-German harassment took many different forms. Members of the Evangelical Association who were young people during World War I can still remember some of the harassment. For example, George Doeden of Worthington Emmanuel recounted in an interview how German-Americans in that area were often harassed into buying more war bonds than they could really afford.[18] Mildred Schroeder from Brush Creek Tabor related how some of the Norwegian-Americans in the area would "goose step" like German soldiers behind German-Americans.[19]

Sometimes the harassment became physically as well as verbally abusive, and sometimes it was carried out in an organized manner. An example of the latter is given by Richard Lunde in his writing about the issue as it affected the Evangelical Association in the Dakotas. He states:

> At least one outsider could be expected to attend every church activity acting as a spy for the other townspeople and for the government. People were always listening at the doors and windows to gather information against the Evangelical Church. In at least one case, the minister of another church was found hiding in the furnace room of the

Evangelical Church during services while his own congregation was waiting for him to conduct their service.[20]

So it is no wonder that the anti-German hysteria during World War I contributed greatly to the transition from German to English, along with pressures from the younger and more assimilated Evangelicals.

German to English in South Central Minnesota

In this area as elsewhere, the language battle was fought out in each individual congregation, as both the state and national conferences felt that this issue was best resolved on the local level. The Evangelical churches clustered in Faribault County were in areas of heavy German settlement, so outside pressures to change to English were not as great. And while the anti-German hysteria of World War I certainly affected German-Americans in Faribault County, it did not result in the abandonment of German in either Lutheran or Evangelical churches there.

As is the case elsewhere, the records are not necessarily clear on precisely when each church changed to English, as it was always a gradual change. Pressures from inside the churches for some English usage were already present before the war, as the children and young people became less and less willing or able to speak, read, or write German. At Blue Earth Salem for example, the minutes of the annual meeting on November 2, 1908 state: "Voted to organize English classes in Sunday School. The parents to decide which class their child shall attend."[21] In 1909 a request was made to the Quarterly Conference to have one Sunday evening service each month in English, and ten years later (in 1919, after World War I had ended) it was decided to hold an alternate Sunday morning service in English. By 1922, it was voted to hold English services every Sunday morning with German services every other Sunday evening, which were changed to two morning services six months later. The records do not indicate exactly when the German services were discontinued, but this account does say that all services at Blue Earth Salem were in English since 1930.[22]

The rural Blue Earth Immanuel Church maintained some German into the early 1920s. Utzinger stated in 1922 that the language question had been settled and that "...all the services are now held in the English language at Immanuel."[23] One might be inclined to think that the rural churches would have held to the German language longer than those in town, since townspeople might be more likely to be interacting with other ethnic groups who spoke English. However, one must also remember that at that time the nuclei of town churches' memberships were older retired people who had moved from the farm into town and were more likely to speak German.

The records do not clearly indicate when the Rice Lake Emmanuel and Brush Creek Tabor churches made the transition to English. Their written records, however, changed gradually from German to English between 1918 and 1927.[24] An interview with life-long Rice Lake member Orville Urbain indicated that there was one service a month in German for a while, with the last one in about 1928.[25]

As for Dunbar Zion, confirmation and Sunday School classes were conducted in German until about 1915. English then gradually replaced German in all services by 1935, when the last German service was conducted by Reverend Moses Schoenleben.[26]

Wells Salem (the town church served with Dunbar Zion), made the transition to English around the same time as Dunbar, but not without much bitterness and dissension. Utzinger states: "The change of the language caused the defection of a number of families, which was much to be regretted."[27] Those who left, among whom were some of Salem's founding families, went to the German Lutheran church in town since their services were still in German.[28] One must assume that for all of those who left, the maintenance of the German language had become more important to them than being an Evangelical, and language had triumphed over doctrine.

In any case, the bitterness lingered for years, with families who left not speaking to those who stayed, and vice versa. This lingering bitterness was still present in the late 1940s. As a small child and daughter of Wells Salem's minister, Reverend Ralph Esterly, I recall wondering why two older ladies who lived nearby would never speak to anyone in our family. I was told that they had left our church over the language issue and still held a grudge against the Evangelicals for switching to English. This shows some of the depth of feeling there was on the language issue both before and long after the transition to English actually took place.

German to English in Western Minnesota

The Evangelical churches in western Minnesota were for the most part similar to those in Faribault County in their transition to English. With one exception, they continued to maintain some German in their services well after World War I, and into the 1920s and even the 1930s. The exception was Madison Ebenezer. This church made the transition perhaps as early as 1905, according to current member William Smith whose parents were early members of this church.[29] It should be remembered that Madison and the surrounding area was a center of Norwegian settlement, so there were Norwegians as well as Germans in the Evangelical Church. A minister at Madison in the 1940s once remarked (perhaps revealing more German chauvinism than he intended): "This is a strange congregation; first of all, it is a church made up of mostly former Norwegian Lutherans."[30]

The other four Evangelical churches in this area, Fairfield Zion, Yellowbank Emmanuel, Salem, and Bellingham Zion, all made a very gradual transition to English. Fairfield Zion maintained some German well into the 1920s, according to a member of that church, Lillian Opp Wendland.[31] The other three churches, (all close together in Lac Qui Parle County), apparently had made some concessions to English by the early 1920s also. Current older members of Bellingham Zion who grew up in that church or in one of the other two nearby churches, all state that they were confirmed in English, not in German, even though German services were still being held. One of these members who grew up in the Bellingham church (Florence Kotke Bombeck) stated that Reverend A. H. Utzinger who came to

Bellingham in 1921, started the first English catechism class. She also says:

> My personal recollection is that we had services in the German language at least through the twenties. However, more importantly, I seem to recall that when the idea was raised of changing to English, many of the older folks had a difficult time with the thought of making the change. Still the change came about because the older members believed the young people were the future of our church. [32]

Another Bellingham member, Helen Gloege Ness, recounted that when Reverend F. W. Schendel first preached in English in the mid-1920s, an elderly German-speaking lady got up and left in a huff. [33] It appears that as in so many other places, the transition to English was accomplished both in spite of and because of members' deeply felt views on the issue.

Some German services were held into the 1930s in these three churches. Salem maintained German until it merged with Bellingham Zion in 1931, having only Sunday School in English in its later years. Yellowbank continued with some German in the 1930s. The last German service in Bellingham Zion was in 1939, on the eve of World War II; it was conducted by Reverend E. M. Schendel.[34] It may well be that the German services would not have ended then, but Bellingham Zion was then sent a minister who spoke no German. It was felt by some at Zion that this was done deliberately to force Zion to drop the last vestiges of German; this cannot be proven but is certainly within the realm of reasonable conjecture.

In looking at why some of the Evangelical churches in western Minnesota were the last to give up German in their services, we need to remember that German immigrants settled in this area ten to twenty years later than those in south central Minnesota. They were in German enclaves like those in south central Minnesota but were not similar to Evangelical churches in southwest Minnesota where there were fewer Germans and the transition to English came sooner. Similar patterns could be seen later in the Dakotas, and western Canada, where later German immigration and heavy concentrations of German settlement resulted in Evangelical churches where some German was maintained even after World War II.

This chapter has so far looked at two major divisive movements within the Evangelical Association between 1891 and 1921. One of these was the split within the denomination, resulting in two separate churches (Evangelical Association and United Evangelical) for almost thirty years. The other was the language issue, which caused hurt and bitterness as it was resolved on the Minnesota prairie and elsewhere.

It is important to know that the transition from German to English in these Evangelical churches was not easy and quick and that it left scars on many congregations. It is even more important to realize that these churches not only survived the trauma of the language transition, but also grew and prospered during this time in spite of those issues.

Change and Growth: 1891 – 1921

These were years of great change and upheaval for the country as a whole, and the turn of the century from nineteenth to twentieth was more than just symbolic. The late nineteenth century saw the closing of the western frontier, and while there were still large numbers of immigrants coming into the United States they were primarily settling in the cities of the East and Midwest and not as much in rural areas.

Industrialization was proceeding at a great rate in the cities, and affected life on the farm and small towns as well. The late nineteenth century was still the age of steam, and gigantic steam tractors huffed and puffed their way across midwestern farm fields. By the end of World War I, gasoline-powered tractors were just beginning to appear on the scene, and by that time also, the automobile was transforming the country. As the use of automobiles spread to rural areas, rural and small town people became less isolated from each other and rural people were able to participate in a wider variety of activities.

More consumer goods were also available, especially with the Sears, Roebuck and Montgomery Ward mail order catalogs offering a variety of goods hitherto virtually unavailable to rural and small town people. The telephone and radio were also factors in broadening communication and spreading knowledge more quickly and easily. Other inventions and improvements (electric lights, indoor plumbing, electric appliances, etc.), began to make their way into the towns and even into some rural areas, and by 1920 these labor-saving devices continued to make their way into more and more areas.

These many changes came at the same time (and not coincidentally) as the Evangelical Association was forced to deal with the change from German to English. These changes, and the wider opportunities they brought with them, meant that the church (of whatever denomination) was no longer the major or only social as well as spiritual center of a community. There were now more competing activities such as motion pictures and automobiles to take people much further for entertainment and social activities. Churches in general (and the Evangelical Association specifically), had to deal with change and with the challenges brought by these changes in order to survive and thrive.

World War I brought economic changes as well to Americans in both urban and rural areas. Providing foodstuffs and other goods to the Allies during and after the war brought comparative prosperity to American farmers. Successful farmers were able to raise their own standard of living, and to purchase goods previously not affordable. Land prices increased in Minnesota and elsewhere, and a fair number of farm families took advantage of this. They sold their current farms at a profit and moved westward, often to Washington or California to purchase new farms there.

South Central Minnesota Churches: 1891-1921

The churches in this area of course faced the changes and challenges discussed above, along with the traumatic and divisive language change. That they managed to survive and generally prosper in spite of all this is a testament to both their ministers and lay people. As the chart below shows, membership in all these churches increased between 1890 and 1921, except in Blue Earth Immanuel where the decline was more than compensated for by the growth in the nearby town church, Blue Earth Salem. Dunbar Zion moved its building two miles in 1891 to be nearer its membership, and Wells Salem built a large new church in 1892. The Blue Earth Salem congregation built its second, and larger, church in 1895 to accommodate its rapidly expanding membership, while Rice Lake Emmanuel enlarged their church in 1907.

Southwestern Minnesota Churches: 1891-1921

As discussed earlier, the language issue and transition to English was less divisive in this area than in south central or western Minnesota. These churches were mostly founded later than those in south central Minnesota, and many of them built their first, or enlarged their older, churches around the turn of the century. Welcome Emmanuel built in 1891, and nearby Fairmont Salem in 1900. Worthington Emmanuel also built in 1891, Steen Salem in 1894, Pipestone Zion (town) in 1898, Marshall Salem in 1900, and Clifton Bethel in 1905. Luverne Ebenezer had built a new church in 1884, which burned down in December 1917. Within a week the basement was excavated, and a new brick building was constructed. It was dedicated on May 25, 1918, not even six months after fire had destroyed their old church;[36] these were not people to let the grass grow under their feet!

As indicated below, there was a lot of building to accommodate growth in this area in the late nineteenth century, in both rural and town churches. Membership in these churches rose between 1890 and 1910, but as the chart below indicates, several of them show a decrease in membership between 1910 and 1921. Some of this decrease may have been due to the language issue, but was more than likely primarily due to farmers selling their farms during and after World War I and buying land on the West Coast. Those who bought these farms in southwest Minnesota were not necessarily, and probably were not, Germans who might be more inclined toward the Evangelical Association.

Church Membership: South Central Minnesota [35]			
Church	1890	1910	1921
Blue Earth Immanuel	208	149	125
Blue Earth Salem	101	226	354
Rice Lake Emmanuel		163	174
Brush Creek Tabor	323		
Dunbar Zion		186	202
Wells Salem			
Totals	632	724	855

Church Membership: Southwestern Minnesota			
Church	1890	1910	1921
Welcome Emmanuel	117	141	94
Fairmont Salem			
Worthington Emmanuel	75	105	87
Luverne Ebenezer	74	98	111
Steen Salem			
Pipestone Salem	67	105	83
Pipestone Zion			
Hendricks Zion	26	55	38
Marshall Salem	57	136	142
Clifton Bethel			
Totals	416	640	555

72

(Chart continued from previous page)

Church Membership: Western Minnesota			
Church	1890	1910	1921
Appleton Circuit (Fairfield & Madison)	67	54	95
Odessa Circuit (Bellingham, Yellowbank, Salem)	274	260	
Bellingham Zion			142
Odessa Circuit (Yellowbank, Salem)			171
Totals	341	314	408
GRAND TOTALS	1389	1678	1818

Western Minnesota Churches: 1891-1921

The language issue was by no means settled by 1921 in many of the churches in western Minnesota, other than in Madison Ebenezer which had made the change by 1905. This was an area with enclaves of German settlement and some use of the German language in these Evangelical churches continued in the 1920s and even into the 1930s.

Before the turn of the century new buildings were put up at Salem in Yellowbank Township in 1893, and Fairfield Zion in 1895. Bellingham Zion had built its first church in 1891, and decided to enlarge and virtually rebuild their church in 1910. The new building was completed and then dedicated debt free on October 23, 1910. An overheated furnace started a fire on January 2, 1911, and the building burned to the ground ten weeks after completion.[37] But before the ashes from the fire were cold, the

73

congregation voted to press forward and rebuild. Their sacrifice and dedication resulted in a new and beautiful church building which was built in the summer of 1911.[38] We sometimes tend to forget the blood, sweat and tears that went into the building of these churches to the glory of God, and it behooves us to remember and to be thankful for these dedicated men and women.

As was true in southwest Minnesota there were those who sold out and moved west, and some of this occurred even before World War I. The Fairfield Zion Church was particularly hard hit. As a history of the Fairfield Sunday School states:

> The congregation was enjoying a steady growth until 1912 when some of our families started to sell out and move to Yakima, Washington. At present there are twelve families who have left Fairfield and gone to Yakima.[39]

The Madison Ebenezer Church also experienced a decline in membership during this time. Apparently this was due more to some members losing interest than their moving away. In fact, disbanding the church entirely was discussed in the early teens. But then a noted evangelist, E.P. Mankofsky, preached in Madison and with local efforts also, the church regrouped, regained lost ground, and remodeled and enlarged their church in 1916.[40]

Membership figures for these western Minnesota churches are shown in the chart above; the Appleton Circuit includes Madison and Fairfield, while the Odessa Circuit included Bellingham, Yellowbank and Salem in 1890 and 1910. By 1921, Bellingham was listed separately from the Odessa Circuit which then included Yellowbank Emmanuel and Salem. Membership for the Odessa United Evangelical Church is not included until this church became part of the reunited Evangelical Church after 1922.

Summary: 1891-1921

As is evident throughout this chapter, these years were years of confrontation and divisiveness for the Evangelical Association on the Minnesota prairie, and elsewhere. The national denominational split resulting in the separate Evangelical Association and the United Evangelical Church did not tear apart Evangelical churches in Minnesota like it did further east in many churches, but it did cause some problems and bitterness, particularly in western Minnesota.

The language issue was of major importance to these Minnesota churches, especially in south central and western Minnesota where some German was maintained in services even into the 1930s. The transition to English left scars in some congregations which took decades to heal. This is not readily apparent in "official" documents. Even in Utzingers' *History of the Minnesota Conference*, which was published in 1922, the language issue is referred to obliquely rather than directly. As in any "official" history, the negatives are downplayed. The length of time it took many churches to make the transition to English, along with numerous recollections of people who were young Evangelicals at the time, lets us know how traumatic and important this issue really was.

With the language issue well on its way to settlement and completion of the transition to English, and with reunification of the Evangelical Association and United Evangelicals into the Evangelical Church in 1922, the future looked bright for Evangelicals in Minnesota and elsewhere. It was a time of optimism and prosperity, and the next chapter will trace the path of the Evangelical Church on the Minnesota prairie from 1922 to the mid-1940s.

Notes

1 Kenneth W. Krueger, "Early Days of the Evangelical Church in the Canadian West, Memories and Reflections," *Telescope-Messenger*, Vol. - 6, No. 1 (Winter 1996), p.5. The "new" *Telescope-Messenger* is published quarterly by the Center for the Evangelical United Brethren Heritage, United Theological Seminary, Dayton,Ohio.

2 *Ibid.*

3 Glenn Esterly, Esterly Family Reunion, Maple Grove Immanuel Church, September 28, 1991.

4 Eller, *These E.U.B.'s*, p.75

5 *Ibid.*

6 Raymond W. Albright, *A History of the Evangelical Church* (Harrisburg, 1942), p. 331.

[7] The Correll and Odessa appointments were not Evangelical appointments until after the 1922 Evangelical Association and United Evangelicals reunification; hence, the Correll appointment is not included in this study. The Odessa appointment *is* included, since it later joined with Yellowbank Emmanuel to form Odessa Hope.

[8] Reuben Yaekel, *History of the Evangelical Association, Vol. 1, 1750-1850* (Cleveland, 1894), p.355.

[9] Elwyn B. Robinson, *History of North Dakota* (Lincoln, 1966), p. 290.

[10] *General Conference Journal,* 1879, p. 25 in Edward F. Ohms, "The Language Problem in the Evangelical Association," *Methodist History* Vol.24, No.4 (July 1987), p. 234.

[11] *Ibid.,* p. 231.

[12] Huelster, *Miracle of Grace,* pp. 473-475.

[13] *Ibid.,* pp. 475-476,

[14] Minnesota United Methodist Conference Records, Box 7, Book 59, Volume 2, Welcome Emmanuel records.

[15] Minnesota United Methodist Conference Records, Box 1, Book 1, Reverend C. G. Roesti, p. 6.

[16] Arthur P. Rose, *An Illustrated History of Nobles County, Minnesota* (Worthington, 1908) p. 209.

[17] *History of the Zion Evangelical United Brethren Church, 75th Anniversary, 1889-1964,* Pipestone Zion records.

[18] George Doeden, Interview of July 12, 1995, Worthington, Minnesota.

[19] Mildred Schroeder, Interview of June 9, 1994, Wells, Minnesota.

[20] Richard M. Lunde, *History of the Evangelical United Brethren Church in the Dakotas* (Grand Forks, 1959) p. 154.

[21] Blue Earth Salem "Centennial Notes," compiled by Freda Berndt, December 1981, p. 1, Blue Earth Salem records.

[22] *Ibid.*

[23] Utzinger, *History of the Minnesota Conference*, p. 343.

[24] *Kirchenbuch Rice Lake Circuit der Minnesota Conferenz der Evangelischen Gemeinschaft, 1902-1942.* (Church Record Book, Rice Lake Circuit of the Minnesota Conference of the Evangelical Association), Rice Lake Emmanuel records.

[25] Orville Urbain, Interview of June 6, 1994, Wells, Minnesota.

[26] Reuben Kaiser, "Dunbar Zion Evangelical Church, 1865-1946," *The United Methodist Church of Wells 125th Anniversary 1865-1990 Observance,* p. 9, Wells records.

[27] Utzinger, *History of the Minnesota Conference*, p. 432.

[28] German Lutherans maintained the German language in their churches much longer, in spite of World War I pressure to make the switch to English. Their church-related schools were instrumental in this, since these schools provided not only instruction in the German language but also some isolation from the larger English-speaking culture.

[29] William Smith, Interview of September 15, 1994, Madison, Minnesota.

[30] Minnesota United Methodist Conference Records, Folder 1, Letter from Reverend C. E. Burkhart to Reverend Roy Heitke, undated.

[31] Lillian Opp Wendland, Interview of September 21, 1994, Bellingham, Minnesota.

[32] Florence Kotke Bombeck, "Memories," *Zion United Methodist Church, 1889-1989*, p. 57, Bellingham Zion records.

[33] Helen Gloege Ness, Interview of September 21, 1994, Bellingham, Minnesota.

[34] *Zion United Methodist Church, 1889-1989*, p.3, Bellingham Zion records.

[35] All membership numbers in charts are taken from the Minnesota Conference Official Records for the years shown.

[36] "Historical Sketch," 1873-1938, *Sixty-fifth Anniversary of the Pleasant View Evangelical Church, 1873-1938*, Luverne Ebenezer (Pleasant View) records.

[37] "Our Church Buildings," *Zion United Methodist Church, 1889-1989*, p. 11, Bellingham Zion records.

[38] *Ibid.*, p. 14.

[39] Minnesota United Methodist Conference Records, Box 1, Folder 1, History of the Fairfield Sunday School, Fairfield Zion records.

[40] Utzinger, *History of the Minnesota Conference*, p. 340.

Chapter Five

Moving Toward the Mainstream:
1922 – 1945

The Evangelical Church at the National Level
Reunification

The official union of the Evangelical Association and the United Evangelicals into the Evangelical Church took place in October 1922 in Detroit, Michigan. It was the culmination of years of hard work by both clergy and lay people, and was supported by most of the members of both groups. There was, however, a minority (about one-fifth) of the United Evangelicals who withdrew and formed the Evangelical Congregational Church. The majority were most enthused about the reunion of the two groups, and as Albright states:

By this happy union the new church now displayed a strength never felt by either body. The membership of the body was 259,417, and there were 419,245 enrolled in the Sunday Schools. The ministers of the denomination numbered 1,856 with an additional 575 in a local part-time relationship. Enthusiasm ran high among those who had labored in these years to accomplish the reuniting of these bodies as well as among the laity throughout all portions of the new church who had caught the vision of the larger responsibilities of the enlarged church united in numbers and in spirit.[1]

Other Merger Possibilities

During these years there was also some interest in other mergers or unions. From 1907 on, there were suggestions for closer cooperation with the Methodists, and in 1911 there was actually a specific proposition for merger with the Methodists. The Methodist delegate to the Evangelical Association's General Conference in 1911 (Reverend John Krantz of New York City) spoke to the assembled delegates, suggesting "... that we might be united into one solidified and unified Evangelical Methodism."[2] But, as Albright stated: "...no definite movement toward an actual merging was ever accomplished, probably because the Evangelicals feared a complete loss of identity in any such union."[3]

There was also some discussion by the mid-1920s of a merger of four denominations with German backgrounds. These were the Reformed Church in the United States, the Evangelical Synod of North America, the Church of the United Brethren in Christ, and the Evangelical Church. The first two had presbyterial (local governance) systems while the latter two were episcopal (governed by bishops), but it was felt by the plan's proponents that the common German background and pietistic tradition of all four denominations would be a sufficient unifying factor. Also, as Behney and Eller point out: " They were of comparable numerical dimension so that the charge could not be raised that any one was absorbing any others."4

The Evangelical Church was not actually involved in the merger discussions. This was because they were still working out their own recent reunification, and probably also because they had some fundamental differences with the Reformed Church and the Evangelical Synod, not the least of which was the Evangelical Church's stand on total abstinence from all alcohol. In any case, the discussions resulted in a "Plan of Union" being adopted by the other three bodies by 1929. This merger did not materialize, but in 1934 the two presbyterial bodies did merge and become the Evangelical and Reformed Church. The Evangelical Church, meanwhile, did pursue a closer relationship with the United Brethren in Christ which would result in a merger of these two bodies in 1946.

Expanding Outreach and Missions

Even while the Evangelical Association's mission was largely still aimed at German-speaking people, missions were also established not only in Canada (to German immigrants), and Switzerland, but also in Alsace-Lorraine in France, China, Japan,

83

and Africa. And in this country, the Evangelical Association established missions to Italian immigrants in Milwaukee, Kenosha and Racine, Wisconsin before World War I. The United Evangelicals established a mission in the Kentucky mountains in 1921, which then became a mission of the Evangelical Church after the 1922 merger.

Clearly the Evangelical Church had gradually broadened its outreach and mission. With the advent of World War I German immigration to the United States virtually ceased, and with the restrictive immigration laws in the 1920s it remained minimal. The German language was maintained longer (up to World War II in some areas) in the Dakotas where more recent German immigrants had settled before World War I. And Germans (many from Russia) who still maintained the German language and culture continued to immigrate to the prairie provinces of Canada. The Evangelical Church established the Northwest Canada Conference in 1927 under the leadership of Dr. W. W. Krueger; this was no doubt the last Evangelical mission for German immigrants in North America.

Evangelicals in Minnesota

Meanwhile in Minnesota, the reunited Evangelical Church had 7,980 members statewide in 1923, and most congregations had completed the transition to the English language by this time. A few, such as Bellingham Zion and Wells Salem still maintained some German through the 1920s and even into the 1930s. As the last chapter indicated, the language issue along with the denominational split in the 1890s were the most divisive issues to confront the Evangelical Church. The denominational split had not impacted Minnesota as much as elsewhere; the language issue certainly did. But the Evangelical Church survived these divisive issues and even prospered.

Lake Koronis Assembly Grounds

As was discussed in earlier chapters, "camp meetings" had always played an important role in Evangelical church life. These "camp" or "bush" meetings were often held in a member's grove, and sometimes became more established as distinct Evangelical campgrounds. In Minnesota, the Yellowbank Campgrounds adjacent to the Yellowbank Emmanuel Church in Lac Qui Parle County was such a place, with camp meetings generally lasting for two weeks in June. Other areas also had specific camp meeting locations.

The Minnesota Conference had been interested for some time in acquiring camp or assembly grounds. With the advent of the automobile, people could now travel much further, and campgrounds did not need to be within range of an hour-or-two horse and buggy ride. They first considered a plan for the three conference districts to each get their own camp meeting grounds, but then decided that one location could serve the whole state. In 1921 there were proposals submitted from Waseca, Faribault, and Paynesville, and the Paynesville/Lake Koronis proposition was unanimously agreed upon.

Paynesville/Lake Koronis was a logical choice, since it was not only a beautiful location, but was also centrally located in Minnesota (see map, p. xxiii). It was also a major Evangelical center, with five Evangelical churches in the immediate area; i.e., Paynesville First (in town) and Salem, Zion, Ebenezer, and Emmanuel (Grove) in the country. These five churches had a combined membership of 628 in 1921.

Building at Lake Koronis began almost immediately, in order to be ready for the State Young People's Alliance and Sunday School Convention in June and July of 1922.[5] A year later, the Board of Directors' first annual report said:

> The attendance and success of these gatherings (the first camp meeting and the first convention) were far beyond our fondest expectations. The fact that our long cherished hopes to have such a place within the bounds of our Conference had at last been realized created an enthusiasm that helped the delegates to overlook the somewhat unfinished condition of the grounds and buildings. We had provided sleeping accommodations for over 100 people and for several nights were crowded to our utmost capacity. The kitchen and dining hall were well managed by our Paynesville Ladies' Aid Society... "The Lord hath done great things for us, whereof we are glad." The total expenditures for grounds, buildings, equipment and improvements up to date amount to $21,892.70.[6]

This obviously enthusiastic and heartfelt assessment of the meaning of the Lake Koronis Assembly Grounds was not confined to the Board of Directors, nor was it transitory.

The Assembly Grounds soon became Minnesota's Evangelical center for camp or evangelistic meetings and Summer Assembly, formerly the Young People's Alliance and Sunday School Convention. The Minnesota Bible Conference and the Leadership Education School both merged with the Summer Assembly, and boys' and girls' camps were also established. In addition to the tabernacle, chapel, and dormitories, several private cottages (many of them owned by Evangelical ministers) were constructed on the grounds. Landscaping and other improvements were added as the need arose.

But the Lake Koronis Assembly Grounds was not just its buildings or its lakeside location; its meaning transcended that description for many, if not most, of those who participated in the Evangelical gatherings there. The youth and adults who attended such gatherings often formed meaningful friendships with others, and a number of young people met their future spouses there. Also, many young men (women were not yet accepted into the ministry) felt called into Christian ministry while at Koronis Assembly. Many were led to a conversion experience, while others of all ages, simply felt that their faith had been strengthened and their horizons broadened through attending camp, Assembly, or other gatherings at Lake Koronis.

In addition to the above-mentioned benefits of the Lake Koronis Assembly Grounds to individuals, it should be noted that the Assembly Grounds and its many programs really helped to create and perpetuate a real Evangelical (and later, Evangelical United Brethren) Center in Minnesota. While many Evangelical lay people had often attended services on "Conference Sunday" on the last day of the annual conference, their attendance at services on "Assembly Sunday" soon eclipsed Conference Sunday attendance. Sunday morning services in the Koronis tabernacle often overflowed onto the adjacent hillside, with hundreds of people in attendance.

After the morning services people spread out over the lake-side Assembly Grounds with their picnic dinners, enjoying the view, the good food, and sharing conversations about past, present, and future. By late afternoon the crowds had dispersed and returned to their homes taking their memories of Koronis with them. Surely there must have been some cold and rainy "Koronis Sundays," but in most everyone's memory these Sundays seem to have always been warm and sunny days. In any case, those lay people, young and old, and ministers alike, who participated in programs at Lake Koronis Assembly Grounds would no doubt agree with the evaluation in the Koronis Director's Report of 1943 which stated:

> God only can tabulate the good that has come to our Conference in spiritual enrichment, evangelical fellowship and unity, as a result of Koronis activities.[7]

Minnesota Evangelicals in the 1920s

There were many issues confronting the Evangelical Church in Minnesota in the 1920s, and these are reflected in the various reports in the Conference Journals. Quite clearly, the church was concerned about what they considered to be a decline of Christian values in American society. For example, in 1921 a Conference Journal report expresses the hope that the Young People's Alliance would provide "... social fellowship, which is to keep them from the unhallowed influence of ungodly society."[8]

In 1922, continued support for Evangelical colleges was urged so that "...the evil influences of Liberalism may be counteracted."[9]

Concerns were also expressed about the theory of evolution being taught in the public schools along with other teachings felt to be atheistic. Sunday baseball, movies, and pleasure trips were seen as desecrating the sacredness of the Sabbath, and the church continued to support the temperance cause and the Volstead Act of 1923 which outlawed the making and consumption of alcoholic beverages in the United States. With cigarette smoking on the increase, especially among young people, the church called on Evangelicals to stay away from this "...filthy, harmful and wasteful habit."[10] In looking at these many concerns, Conference leadership stressed the need for more evangelistic endeavors by Evangelical churches, and a conference report in 1929 stated:

> As we study the situation we are more and more convinced that our salvation lies not in retrenchment nor amalgamation, but in a real Conference-wide thorough going revival.[11]

While the above discussion might sound like Evangelicals were interested only in issues related to personal salvation, this was not so. The church also expressed concerns about social issues. They specifically spoke out against war, stating in 1925:

> ...We, as the Minnesota Conference of the Evangelical Church, take a definite stand against war, refusing to give it the sanction and blessing of the Church.[12]

In addition to support for a general outlawing of war they expressed support for the establishment of a World Court.

Rural/Urban Issues and Evangelical Expansion In Minnesota

Perhaps the most important way in which the Evangelical Church sought to expand its outreach was in its realization that this still primarily rural and small town based church would also need to increase its work in larger cities. This was already being discussed on a national level by the turn of the century. But as Behney and Eller point out, "...this thrust toward cities was greeted with less than enthusiasm in some quarters," and there was concern about losing "...our genius for rural evangelism."[13] Continuing to work in rural areas and to better cope with rural problems was still seen as very important.

In any case, this issue of Evangelical expansion into urban areas reached into Minnesota as well. A mission church (Calvary) was started in St. Paul in 1913, and a handsome brick church was built in 1921. In Minneapolis, Oakland Avenue Church was founded in 1921, in an area developing on the South Side where several former members of First Church in North Minneapolis had moved. In Duluth, when a mission church began in 1896 finally failed, a new church (Chester Park) was beginning and a new building was completed in 1928. Other than the nucleus of old German Evangelicals at Oakland Avenue Church, it should be noted that these new churches were reaching out to people in new neighborhoods and not just to those of German origin.

The Presiding Elders' (later, District/Conference Superintendent) Report of 1929 is a clear statement of this new emphasis to be coupled with old Evangelical methods in these impassioned remarks appearing in the Conference Journal:

Through personal evangelism and protracted meetings, fired by a real missionary spirit, our congregations were established. We had only one barrier in those days. Language was our only boundary. Because of it we are not in many places today where we ought to be. Minneapolis ought to have more Evangelical congregations. St. Paul has unchurched communities. We should have been in places like Albert Lea, Owatonna, Red Wing, Northfield and scores of others. Our present day city churches ought to have twice and three times the membership they now have.[14]

Minnesota Ministers

As the Evangelical Church worked to broaden its outreach into larger towns and cities in Minnesota, so too were changes taking place in the church's ministers. On a national level the last decades of the nineteenth century saw an increasing emphasis on general education and seminary training for Evangelical ministers. This emphasis did not negate or diminish (as some early leaders felt it might) the church's firm belief that its ministers must first and foremost feel called by God into Christian ministry. Education and particularly some seminary training were thus seen as a way of enhancing the ministry of the church.

In Minnesota, as elsewhere, early Evangelical ministers were overwhelmingly of rural farming backgrounds. Many of them had farmed for some time before entering the ministry; in earlier years a fair number of them continued to do some farming off and on during their years in the ministry. Educational levels of the

91

ministers varied greatly, from their having attended a few primary grades in the United States to some college or seminary training in the United States or in Germany.

In order to try to deal with this wide variation the various conferences early on set up courses of study and examinations for ministerial candidates in order to ensure that all Evangelical ministers were adequately prepared. The course of study for the Minnesota Conference in 1921 included such topics as History of the Evangelical Association, Old Testament Theology, History of Missions, The Preacher and His Life Work, and Preparation and Delivery of Sermons.[15] Clearly ministerial candidates were expected to spend a good deal of time and effort completing it.

Completing such a course of study along with making a living and perhaps supporting a wife and children was not easy, and often required great sacrifices. Few, if any, of these aspiring ministers came from wealthy backgrounds but generally they were used to hard work from an early age, having grown up on farms.

During the years between World Wars I and II, more and more of those entering the ministry were able to finish high school and go on to higher education. It must be remembered, however, that a high school diploma, much less a college degree, was not the usual expectation at that time. It was particularly difficult for those living in rural areas, as they usually had to move into or stay in town during the week to attend high school.

Some information about my own family on this subject illustrates what getting an education meant in the early decades of the twentieth century. My father's family, the Esterly's, lived on a farm near Hanover, Minnesota, about forty miles northwest of

Minneapolis. Forty miles in those days was more like 400 miles would be today. My Aunt Sarah (Sarah Esterly Howard, 1898-1995) was the first person from Hanover to go in to Minneapolis to attend high school. Her mother (Emma Esterly, 1873-1961) supported her in this venture, while her father (Henry Esterly, 1865-1945) was opposed on the grounds that a high school diploma would be of no use (particularly to a girl) and anyway, she was needed on the farm. This viewpoint was no doubt the more accepted one in that culture. However, Sarah and her mother prevailed, and Sarah graduated with honors from Minneapolis North High School in 1918 while working as a live-in maid and nanny.

Sarah's having made the move into the city made it easier for two of her younger brothers, who also wanted to go to high school. So while two brothers, Jess and Fred, stayed in farming, the two younger brothers, Wes and my father Ralph (1906-1958), were able to live with Sarah and her husband while attending high school. Their parents, Henry and Emma Esterly, then also moved into Minneapolis due to Henry's ill-health, so my father was able to live at home while working full time, and after high school graduation, to attend the University of Minnesota along with his brother Wes. Wes received his law degree in 1928, the same year my father received his bachelor's degree. Ralph then moved on to Evangelical Theological Seminary in Naperville, Illinois. Taking one year off to work as a student minister because he needed money to finish seminary, he graduated in 1932.

One of my fathers' classmates at seminary was his first cousin, Ervin (E. M.) Schendel, who grew up on the farm next to the Esterly's; Ervin's mother was Emma Esterly Schendel. Ervin was born in 1898, and was thus in the same class as his cousin Sarah. After eighth grade, he was expected to work on the family farm, and he did so until he felt called into the Christian ministry. He then attended the Academy, (a high school curriculum available through the Evangelical Church's North Western College (now North Central College) in Naperville, Illinois, to complete high school. He went on to North Central College, graduating in 1930, and then graduated from Evangelical Theological Seminary in 1932, at the age of 34.

The stories of these two Evangelical ministers, Ralph Esterly and Ervin Schendel, both called from the Hanover Zion congregation, were not the exception. They were fairly typical of those entering the ministry in those years. Many, if not most of them, made considerable sacrifices preparing for their life's work. The Minnesota Conference was becoming more adamant about its ministers being well-trained, as is seen in the Presiding Elders' Report of 1931 addressing this issue in no uncertain terms, as follows:

> The year has shown us again that the work of the ministry is becoming more and more strenuous, and demands the greatest of qualifications... As a Conference we should be more specific and exacting with our requirements...Our men ought to have no less than a Seminary training, and that preferably in our own Seminary. This includes a thorough high-school course by way of preparation, and better still if they have college training.[16]

Obviously Conference leadership needed and wanted more and more ministers who could be called upon to serve diverse congregations during their ministry. Two good examples are the ministers described above, who while having taken different routes, both graduated from Evangelical Theological Seminary in 1932, and served rural, small town, and city congregations during the course of their ministries. Ralph Esterly served the following fields from 1932 until his death in 1958: Duluth Chester Park, Winona, Wells/Dunbar, and St. Paul Faith. Ervin (E. M.) Schendel served the following fields between 1932 and 1966: Kasson/Sargent, Bellingham, Rochester First, Hutchinson, Blue Earth Salem, Waseca, and Sleepy Eye.

The Prairie Churches in the 1920s

The Evangelical churches in the three areas of south central, southwestern and western Minnesota were more than likely not affected very directly in these years by the Conference's new emphasis on expansion into larger towns and cities. These were not only busy and active years for these churches, they were also quite prosperous years for many people, although this prosperity did not necessarily extend to all farmers and their families. Prices paid to farmers did not keep pace with the prices of consumer goods, and most farmers had become more dependent on goods such as automobiles, that they did not produce.[17]

Rural people were not as isolated as in pre-World War I times, and some, but by no means all, rural churches began to lose membership. Membership loss was due to some members moving away, and also to some choosing to go into a larger town church. But some rural congregations even expanded and/or remodeled their church buildings during the 1920s. Among these were Welcome Emmanuel, where the old church was both expanded and remodeled in 1924. The Rice Lake Emmanuel congregation also remodeled in 1927, adding a basement and removing the old steeple.

The Hendricks Zion (New Grove) congregation also decided to rebuild and enlarge their church building in 1927. A new wing and basement were added, but when almost completed it was burned to the ground on October 11, 1927. As the New Grove church history puts it:

> Even as plans were being made for the dedication of the remodeled and enlarged structure one fall night a fire like a spontaneous combustion raced through the edifice leaving standing only the chimney. One year later, through doubled efforts of members and the building committee, a completely new structure was ready for dedication in November.[18]

The Minnesota Conference offered a donation of $2000 if the new church would be built in the town of Hendricks but this offer was rejected by the congregation in favor of staying in the country.[19] The congregation rebuilt on the old site in 1928, four miles south and one mile east of the town of Hendricks.

Two of the Evangelical churches in towns also rebuilt during the 1920s. Worthington Emmanuel built a new brick church in 1923, while Wells Salem enlarged and remodeled their church in 1926. It is interesting to note how church architectural styles were changing. The new or remodeled churches of the 1920s no longer had tall steeples or spires; this was partially due to wanting a more "modern" look, but also tall steeples on the open prairie tended to attract lightning strikes since they were often the tallest target around whether in town or in the country.

The 1930s: Depression and Retrenchment

The general prosperity and optimism of the 1920s ended with the onset of the Great Depression in October 1929. The early 1930s were years of industrial collapse, widespread unemployment and farm foreclosures. Problems for many midwestern farmers were made much worse by the terrible dust storms which swept across the plains from the Dakotas down to Texas. Many farm families in these areas lost what little they had when their farms were foreclosed, and headed for the West Coast with all their worldly goods in a car or wagon. There was seldom a pot of gold at the end of the rainbow and much like the many laid-off industrial workers from the cities who "rode the rails" looking for work, little work was to be had.

The election of Franklin D. Roosevelt to the presidency of the United States in 1932 brought the advent of the "New Deal" and its many programs. Whether or not one agreed with the philosophy of the New Deal, a sense of hope was one of its main benefits. The economy gradually improved in the later 1930s, but the upturn was not really very obvious until after World War II began in Europe in 1939.

Minnesota Evangelicals in the 1930s

Minnesota farmers were not as hard hit by the dust storms as were those in the Dakotas in the 1930s, but the effects of the Great Depresion were still devastating throughout the state. The drought in western Minnesota was particularly devastating. Naturally the effects were felt also in the churches, and congregations often had to struggle to pay the minister's salary (and were sometimes of necessity late in doing so), or to make needed repairs to the churches and parsonages.

Conference reports certainly acknowledged the problems of the Depression, but also tried to exhort Evangelicals, ministers and lay people alike, to higher levels of commitment and evangelism. The 1936 Report of the District Superintendents addresses this very powerfully, stating:

> Oh, that God might be gracious to our belabored Zion, and if need be, smite with the hammer of deep conviction again among the children of a people whose fathers testified of change which broke the power of evil![20]

The same report also addresses the issues of peace and war. The anti-war pacifist movement was widespread in the 1930s and Evangelical leadership in Minnesota was very clear on this issue, stating:

> ... we whole-heartedly support the young people of our church in voicing their conscientious objection to either actively or passively participating in any armed conflict.[21]

The 1937 Report of the District Superintendents addresses

another issue, that of ethnic diversity within the Evangelical Church in Minnesota. They point out:

It is made up of a dozen or more different nationalities. These many different nationalities with various church backgrounds blend beautifully in most places. In some congregations the melting is still in progress.[22]

They also refer to "respective groups of Germans with a liberal sprinkling of folk of other national and church backgrounds."[23]

The Prairie Churches in the 1930s and early 1940s

The three groups of churches in south central, southwestern and western Minnesota did not reflect the level of ethnic diversity discussed above. Those in southwestern Minnesota (Fairmont west to Luverne and north to Hendricks) were the most diverse of the three groups. As was mentioned in an earlier chapter, this area became home to several different ethnic groups. And while the Evangelical churches in this area were still of predominantly German background, some of them, such as Marshall Salem and Clifton Bethel were more diverse. Others, including most of the rural churches in this area continued to be made up of close-knit family groups of German background.

Evangelical churches in the other two areas (south central and western Minnesota) still reflected their German heritage, with only a small percentage of members from other ethnic groups. These were generally also northern European, such as Norwegian, who had most likely married a German Evangelical, although this was not always the case.

99

Evangelical churches in both south central and western Minnesota (and some in southwestern Minnesota as well) were not only located in areas of German settlement. Church members were also very often related to each other by blood or marriage, and these family groups lived in close proximity to each other. This was particularly true of the rural churches, and while it perpetuated closely-knit church communities, some of them were not very interested in reaching out to other groups of people. Even when they were perfectly willing to try to attract new members from a different heritage it was not easy since any new people in the area often already had another religious preference.

Obviously the Evangelical churches in all three areas, as well as in the rest of Minnesota, did not engage in building programs during the worst years of the Great Depression. Churches were satisfied if they could maintain their buildings, much less build new ones. In fact, two rural churches in western Minnesota closed due to dwindling membership. One of these was Salem Church near Bellingham, which closed in 1931 and merged with Bellingham Zion. The other was Fairfield Zion where many members had been lost to earlier West Coast migration. Fairfield did not officially merge with another church when it closed in 1940; most of its members transferred to the Methodist Church in nearby Appleton.

The rural Blue Earth Immanuel Church did some remodeling in 1940, when they had to move their church back from a new highway. Also, the Madison Ebenezer Church made a longer move, into the town of Madison from its rural location four miles from town. This was in 1940, and an addition was made to the church building at that time as well. It might also be noted here that the Hendricks Zion Church installed an indoor bathroom in the parsonage in 1942.[24] This may seem insignificant to people today, but anyone who experienced Minnesota winters prior to the advent of indoor plumbing would appreciate the importance of such an addition to the parsonage.

The only other building project in these years was at Blue Earth Salem; this was a major project. The congregation had been gathering funds for a new building since 1935. In 1939 they began a three year fund-raising project to build a new church in 1942, but World War II government restrictions temporarily halted further work. Reverend Harley Hiller, minister at Salem, had to meet with the War Production Board in Washington, D. C. in order to get approval for the building project to continue.[25] The lovely new church was then built in the next few months and was dedicated in November 1942.

Membership figures for the three areas for 1930 and 1940 are shown below. The most notable information to be seen here is that while the total membership in both south central and southwestern Minnesota showed a marked increase between 1930 and 1940, there was a slight but very important decrease in the total membership of the churches in western Minnesota. The migration from this region to first the West Coast and then to larger towns and cities in Minnesota or the Dakota's had already begun, as farms in this area began to increase in size, forcing displaced farmers to go elsewhere to find work.

Church Membership: South Central Minnesota

Church	1930	1940
Blue Earth Immanuel	144	120
Blue Earth Salem	294	408
Rice Lake Emmanuel	183	159
Brush Creek Tabor		30
Wells Salem	181	156
Dunbar Zion		108
Totals	802	981

Church Membership: Southwest Minnesota

Church	1930	1940
Fairmont Salem	141	100
Welcome Emmanuel		71
Worthington Emmanuel	143	146
Luverne Ebenezer	105	61
Steen Salem		60
Pipestone Salem	109	82
Pipestone Zion		92
Hendricks Zion	59	71
Marshall Salem	145	104
Clifton Bethel		48
Totals	702	835

Church Membership: Western Minnesota

Church	1930	1940
Madison Ebenezer	39	51
Bellingham Zion	210	180
Salem (YB Twp.)		Closed in 1931
Yellowbank Emmanuel	178	61
Odessa Salem		110
Fairfield Zion	30	27
Totals	457	429
GRAND TOTALS	1961	2245

102

Rural/Urban Issues Revisited

During the years that this chapter covers, it can be seen that there was a gradual shift in emphasis by the Minnesota Conference leadership toward a more urban mission. The Church was trying to meet new challenges as it perceived them. This is not to say, however, that Conference leadership was not also involved with rural churches and their particular concerns. These concerns are addressed very thoughtfully in the District Superintendents' Report of 1941, as follows:

> Our Church in Minnesota is very largely rural. Only about six out of the ninety-two congregations do not now draw from the rural districts for their Church membership. About fifty of over sixty-two men serving fields are of rural church background. This should well qualify us to solve any rural church problem that we may have. The fact is, however, that a philosophy is current that militates against the fields at which altars many of us were converted and against the congregations which have recommended us to the holy ministry. And there is a tendency to look down upon the man who serves the rural church as though he ranks so much lower because he ministers in these communities. The result is the neglect of the rural church and obviously a decrease in membership, interest and enthusiasm...
>
> One realizes a program that has been too much city-conceived and city-centered is difficult to apply and hard to digest in rural areas, and as a result it is thrown into the waste basket as useless and unworkable... Special attention to our rural churches needs to be given. The program built

103

must have in mind the needs of the rural church. The rural churches need to be helped above the inferiority complex which is theirs. They deserve a lifting to a new pride in themselves and to an appreciation in their own inherent worth...we can ill afford, however, to think that anything is good enough for the rural church or consider closing of them as fast as possible.[26]

The above remarks certainly illustrate the desire to be supportive of rural churches. The report goes on, however, to urge churches to be more receptive to change, stating:

It is true that probably the greatest obstacle lies in the characteristic weakness of rural folks, their inability or refusal to meet change with change in the rural church life of our day. We mean to say that a vital Church program for every Church and specifically appropriate for the rural church must be born out of and undergirded by a recognition and appreciation of rural values and rural needs. This will result in spirit led and spirit enabled individuals, ministers and laymen, giving themselves to its working functions.[27]

One may or may not agree with the remarks quoted above. What is of most importance is that the issues were recognized and brought to the table so that they could be hopefully dealt with and not ignored. These were among the prominent issues confronting Minnesota Evangelicals in the early 1940s. They would become even more relevant in post-war years, along with the forthcoming national union with the Church of the United Brethren in Christ, to be discussed in the next chapter.

Notes

[1] Albright, *A History of the Evangelical Church*, p. 388-389.

[2] John Krantz in Albright, p. 389-390.

[3] *Ibid.*, p. 390.

[4] J. Bruce Behney and Paul H. Eller, *The History of the Evangelical United Brethren Church* (Nashville, 1979), p. 277.

[5] Roy S. Heitke, "Historical Summary of the Minnesota Conference (Ev) of the Evangelical United Brethren Church from 1922 to 1951," *Minnesota Conference (Ev) Official Record–1951 (Harrisburg, 1951)*, p. 128.

[6] *Ibid.*

[7] *Ibid.*, p. 129.

[8] *Minnesota Conference Official Record–1921* (St. Paul, 1921), p. 54.

[9] *Minnesota Conference Official Record–1922* (St. Paul, 1922), p. 51.

[10] *Minnesota Conference Official Record–1923* (St. Paul, 1923), p. 48.

[11] *Minnesota Conference Official Record–1929* (St. Cloud, 1929), pp. 70-71.

[12] *Minnesota Conference Official Record–1925* (Waseca, 1925), p. 63.

[13] Behney and Eller, *The History of the EUB Church*, p. 295.

[14] *Minnesota Conference Official Record–1929* (St. Cloud, 1929), p. 71.

[15] *Minnesota Conference Official Record–1922* (St. Paul, 1922), p. 75.

[16] *Minnesota Conference Official Record–1931* (Minneapolis, 1931), p. 78.

[17] David B. Danbom, *Born in the Country: A History of Rural America* (Baltimore, 1995), pp. 188-189.

[18] Mrs. Charles Luekens, "New Grove Zion Evangelical Church," (1969), p. 2, Hendricks Zion (New Grove) records.

[19] "New Grove E.U.B. Church History," p. 4, Hendricks Zion (New Grove) records.

[20] *Minnesota Conference Official Record–1936* (Harrisburg, 1936), p. 49.

[21] *Ibid.*, p. 70.

[22] *Minnesota Conference Official Record–1937* (Harrisburg, 1937), p. 55.

[23] *Ibid.*

[24] *Minnesota Conference Official Record–1942* (Harrisburg, 1942), p. 103.

[25] *Centennial Anniversary, Salem United Methodist Church, 1881-1991,* p. 16, Blue Earth Salem records.

[26] *Minnesota Conference Official Record–1941* (Harrisburg, 1941), pp. 97-98.

[27] *Ibid.*, pp. 98-99.

1. Dunbar Zion, 1874

2. Wells Salem, 1892

3. Wells Salem, Remodeled 1926

4. Wells Salem, 1957

5. Rice Lake Emmanuel, 1880

6. Rice Lake Emmanuel, Remodeled 1907

7. Rice Lake Emmanuel, Remodeled 1927

8. Rice Lake Emmanuel, Remodeled 1951

9. Brush Creek Tabor, 1887

10. Blue Earth Immanuel, 1887

11. Blue Earth Immanuel, 1887 (without steeple)

12. Blue Earth Immanuel, Remodeled 1940

13. Blue Earth Salem, 1881

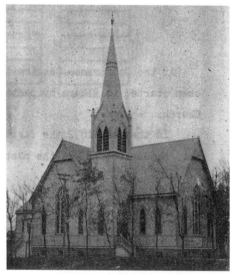

14. Blue Earth Salem, 1895

15. Blue Earth Salem, 1895 (without steeple)

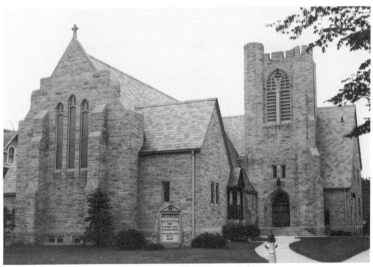

16. Blue Earth Salem, 1942

17.   Fairmont Salem, 1900

18.   Welcome Emmanuel, 1891

19.   Welcome Emmanuel, Remodeled 1924

20. Worthington Emmanuel, 1891

21. Worthington Emmanuel, 1923

22. Luverne Ebenezer (Pleasant View), 1884

23. Luverne Ebenezer (Pleasant View), 1918

24. Luverne Ebenezer (Relocated in Town), 1955

25. Steen Salem, 1894

26. Pipestone Salem, 1899

27. Pipestone Zion, 1898

28. Pipestone Zion, 1960

29.　Hendricks Zion (New Grove), 1884

30.　Hendricks Zion (New Grove), 1928

31. Clifton Bethel, 1905

32. Marshall Salem, 1900

33. Marshall Salem, 1954

34. Madison Ebenezer, 1889

35. Madison Ebenezer, 1916

36. Bellingham Zion, 1891

37. Bellingham Zion, Remodeled, 1910

38. Bellingham Zion, 1911

39.   Salem (Yellowbank Twp.), 1893

40.   Yellowbank Emmanuel, 1881

41. Odessa Salem, 1897

42. Fairfield Zion, 1895

Chapter Six

E.U.B. Union and New Mission Churches
1946 – 1960

Movement Toward Union with the United Brethren

As was noted in the last chapter, there had been some discussion of a four denomination merger in the 1920s, involving the Evangelical Synod, the Reformed Church, the United Brethren in Christ, and the Evangelical Church. The first two denominations, (Evangelical Synod and the Reformed), joined and became the Evangelical and Reformed Church in 1934. The United Brethren in Christ and the Evangelical Church did not pursue that merger but continued to relate closely to each other in the 1920s.

These were years when the Evangelical Church was working hard to solidify its own 1922 union of the Evangelical Association and the United Evangelicals as well as completing the practical and emotional transition from German to English. By the early 1930s the Evangelicals were ready to pursue negotiations with the United Brethren with eventual union of the two denominations as the goal.

During the next eight years (1934-1942) the various appointed groups of the two denominations worked on resolving the issues dividing them. These appear to have been more procedural than doctrinal in nature, involving such issues as ministerial orders, conference organization, pension plans, and publishing and educational institutions. There were also some differences regarding the Confession or Articles of Faith of the two denominations which required compromise, and agreement was gradually reached on this and other issues dividing the denominations.[1] One of these was ordination of women, since the United Brethren had licensed women as ordained ministers since 1889.[2] The United Brethren accepted the Evangelical policy of "men only" in the ordained ministry and while those already ordained would be accepted in the new denomination, no further ordinations of women would occur.

The two denominations had had very similar backgrounds (see Chapter One) and a common Germanic inheritance. The United Brethren, however, had been much quicker to move from the German language to English. This could be seen as an advantage in that it allowed the United Brethren a much larger field of operation; it could be seen as a disadvantage in that they had to compete with other American English-speaking denominations. The Evangelicals, on the other hand, had the advantage of expanding into areas of specific German settlement and competing only with the other German-speaking denominations. This was also a disadvantage in that it limited them to that group only well into the twentieth century.

The two denominations had followed somewhat different paths, but were on most essentials very similar. With regard to size, in 1940 national Evangelical Church membership was 242, 128 while the United Brethren had 421,689 members.[3] The path to union and merger was one of "...unhurried progress... which allowed churchmen at every level to learn of the issues at stake and their resolution."[4]

The Basis of Union was overwhelmingly approved by the General Conference of the Evangelical Church in 1942, and by the United Brethren in 1945. The annual conferences of both denominations also approved the Basis of Union, and the new Evangelical United Brethren Church came into being on November 16, 1946 in Johnstown, Pennsylvania. The new denomination was composed of 4,702 churches and a total membership of 705,102.[5]

Evangelical United Brethren in Minnesota

The national union of Evangelicals and United Brethren into the Evangelical United Brethren Church in 1946 did not really have a momentous effect on the former Evangelical churches in Minnesota. There were two major reasons for this: (1) the Evangelical Church was much larger than the United Brethren in Minnesota, and (2) the conferences of the two denominations did not actually merge until 1951, thus giving them time to solve problems and work through issues in an orderly and thoughtful way.

When the two conferences officially joined in Minnesota in 1951, the Evangelicals had 12,097 members in 87 churches[6] while the United Brethren had 2,235 members in 15 churches.[7] Thus there were more than five times as many Evangelicals as there were United Brethren in the Minnesota Conference. Ten of the fifteen United Brethren churches had 120 or fewer members and were located in the country. Three of the remaining five had between 161 and 200 members, and the two largest (Minneapolis Grace and Rochester East Side, later Homestead Memorial) accounted for 534 and 426 respectively, or almost half of the total of 2,235 United Brethren.[8] The only United Brethren churches located in the areas in this study were in Kiester and Pleasant Prairie (near Winnebago), both in Faribault County. They are not included in the study, since they were not Evangelical appointments in 1922.

The transition in Minnesota to the new Evangelical United Brethren Church was probably felt most keenly by the United Brethren since they were so much smaller. Instead of being part of a very small conference they were now part of a much larger conference which could provide more opportunities but also perhaps less closeness. While the Evangelical contingent was much larger, it appears that the gradual transition to a unified Evangelical United Brethren Conference by 1951 was ably and graciously carried out in Minnesota.

Post War Movement in Minnesota

As was indicated in the last chapter, Minnesota was already experiencing some population shifts by the early 1940s. There had been some population shifts in the state away from rural areas into more urban ones. This was evident first in far western Minnesota, where farms were gradually becoming larger, forcing those displaced to move elsewhere into towns nearby or even to the metropolitan area of Minneapolis and St. Paul.

This population shift was greatly accelerated after World War II ended, with many returning veterans joining others displaced from small farms in moves to new suburban developments. What had been a trickle of movement before World War II became a steady stream during the war years and a veritable torrent in the years following the war. It was not that rural and small town areas all over Minnesota lost population in these post-war years; rather, it was that the great majority of increases in new economic development and subsequently in population growth took place in the Twin Cities and suburbs. Small towns and rural areas were for the most part thriving because their products and services were in demand. So, during these post-war years (1946-1960) many small towns and rural areas were very optimistic, and were certainly not looking ahead to a bleak future.

Churches and the Suburbs, 1946-1950

As more people moved into the new suburban areas around the Twin Cities in Minnesota, the churches of large and small denominations alike saw the need for establishing churches in these areas. Naturally, each denomination wanted to stake out claims for their own group, and there was considerable "vying for position" in new suburban neighborhoods. It became expedient for the Minneapolis Church Federation to develop some guidelines for starting new churches in these areas, so that denominations would not be squabbling with each other over territorial claims. The Federation's Comity Committee took requests for specific territories or neighborhoods from the various denominations, and then assigned areas as equitably as possible. Naturally, not all of their decisions were accepted with equanimity by all concerned, but on the whole the process seems to have worked quite well. Also, there were denominations which did not belong to the Federation, and who then built churches where and when they chose.

Minnesota Evangelicals/E.U.B.'s: 1946-1950

As the last chapter made clear, the Minnesota Conference leadership was already thoughtfully addressing urban/rural issues. After the war, as movement into the suburbs increased dramatically, Evangelicals and then as of 1946/1951 Evangelical United Brethren leadership felt impelled to act decisively to make their denomination visible in the suburbs. As a relatively small denomination without instant "name recognition," they realized they might face an uphill battle in gaining a foothold in these new communities. So it was important for the Conference to put in requests to the Comity Committee for particular suburban neighborhoods without delay.[9]

The two areas granted to the Minnesota E.U.B. Conference by 1947 were in the suburbs of Robbinsdale (bordering Minneapolis on the west) and Richfield (bordering Minneapolis on the south).[10] Since housing was going up very rapidly in Robbinsdale, it was decided that this (Robbinsdale) would be the first Minnesota Conference Missionary Expansion Project, with Richfield to follow later.

It was clear to the leadership of the Minnesota Conference that these "missionary expansion" undertakings would require great commitment and sacrifices from the Conference as a whole. The days were gone when new congregations supplied the materials and then built their churches with their own hands. Money would have to be pledged and paid into building funds to get these projects off the ground, and this would be no easy task. Various pitfalls and problems beset the Robbinsdale project in particular, and while this and other later mission projects were often exciting and inspirational, they must sometimes have seemed also to be incredible leaps of faith.

Support for Suburban Missionary Expansion Projects

Certainly there was much support around the state for these missionary expansion projects, but reports of the Conference Superintendents and others during these years also reflect concerns in this area. The 1949 Conference Superintendents' Report put forth this challenge when discussing the Olivet mission at Robbinsdale:

> We are faced with a great challenge to evangelize such new communities that are springing up in the suburban areas of our metropolitan centers. We must have the missionary spirit to reach out and establish new units of work here in our state. It is sobering to think of the fact that no new unit of our Church has been established in the State of Minnesota since the beginning of the Oakland Avenue

113

Church in Minneapolis in 1920... We pray that the missionary and adventurous spirit of the pioneer fathers may fall upon us to the end that new units of work may be established and that the influence and outreach of our Church may be extended in this State.[11]

And regarding financial support of Conference programs, there is this unambiguous statement from Director of Stewardship, D.C. Trapp, in 1948:

With all the additional cash in circulation today we must remember the old adage that when a man gets rich either God gets a partner or the man loses his soul. Our giving today has not kept pace with $3.00 wheat.[12]

Taking on these missionary expansion projects was a very major undertaking for a relatively small conference; there were 11,692 E.U.B.'s in Minnesota in 1947.[13] Also there may have been other reasons why it was sometimes difficult to raise funds for these new suburban churches.

Historically the Evangelical/E.U.B. Church had its roots in rural and small town areas. This had begun to change before World War I when automobiles made it unnecessary for churches to be located within horse and buggy distance from their parishioners. And by the early 1940s Conference leadership was clearly aware of the growing importance and relevance of urban/rural issues. That did not necessarily mean, however, that rural/small town Evangelicals perceived these issues in the same way.

So while some rural/small town Evangelicals/E.U.B.'s may have been enthused about Conference beginning new churches in the growing suburbs, there were some who viewed these new ventures with mixed feelings. Many of them (in the 1940s and later also) did not have family or friends who lived in or near the Twin Cities and/or they went there rarely themselves. Hence they didn't feel "related" to the Cities, and sometimes felt alienated from them. Also, many of these people still felt very close to their own family and church pioneer past; this was particularly true in far western Minnesota where settlement was in the last quarter of the nineteenth century. Thus, their churches had been built within the living memory of the older people, and in that era churches had more than likely been built by the members themselves. Hence, being asked to help finance the building of churches in the Twin Cities may have seemed a trifle odd to them.

Not actually seeing the new suburban developments personally, as did Conference leadership and others in and near the Cities, no doubt made it more difficult for some rural/small town people to sense the urgency to act swiftly in laying claim to particular suburban neighborhoods. Also, these were years of some growth and change for many of the non-urban churches and there may have been some feeling that missionary expansion funds could have gone to these areas instead.

The Prairie Churches in the Post War 1940s

The post-war 1940s were by and large good years for the prairie churches. In Minnesota as throughout the nation, the early post-war years were the beginning of a period of growth in church membership. In south central Minnesota the rural Dunbar Zion Church (served jointly with Wells Salem) was proceeding with plans to build a new church building. Dunbar was located seven miles from Wells, in open country, and was thus truly a rural church. Its 120 members in 1946 felt confident that they could raise the money to build and sustain a new church which could serve their rural community more effectively than the old building erected in 1874. Other churches in the area (Faribault County) were planning improvements as well, such as the new parsonage planned by Blue Earth Immanuel.

There were also some changes in the works in some of the churches in southwest Minnesota. Luverne was being discussed as a missionary expansion project, and in 1945 a committee was set up to survey prospects in this area. The Luverne church, (Pleasant View Ebenezer), and the parsonage were located six miles from the town of Luverne, and the ministers there also served the Steen Salem Church. On completion of its work the survey committee submitted a report, and the Conference Administrative Council then stated that they sensed "...the urgent necessity to take steps to relocate the church into the city of Luverne..."[14] They also urged that the parsonage should be relocated in Luverne, and authorized some loan and appropriation money toward these relocations.[15] The Pleasant View congregation duly voted in favor of this relocation; however it is quite clear that the impetus and enthusiasm for this move came primarily from the Conference and not the local level. A new parsonage was built in town in 1948, while the church building did not quickly proceed.

In 1946 the Welcome Emmanuel Church was encouraged to relocate in town. This church, served as a joint charge with

Fairmont Salem, was located just two miles from the town of Welcome. This did not result in a move, but the church building's basement was enlarged to provide more Sunday School space. In Marshall the survey committee which was requested by the Marshall Salem and Clifton Bethel churches resulted in the recommendation that the two churches unite and relocate. The Clifton church, with a membership of 56, merged with the Marshall church in 1947 at which time a building program was also launched.

In western Minnesota, where the general population had already begun to decline, the four remaining churches were holding their own but were not considering major building projects at this time. However, in 1945 the town of Ortonville was mentioned as a possible field for missionary expansion, and in 1948 a Conference committee was appointed to survey Ortonville to help determine if this was advisable. Ortonville with a population of 2,469 in 1940,[16] was the largest town in Big Stone County. There were other nearby Evangelical churches located in the village of Odessa in Big Stone County, in Bellingham and in rural Yellowbank Township in Lac Qui Parle County, as well as the Big Stone City Tabor Evangelical Church located just across the Minnesota River in South Dakota. It has already been noted that Conference was encouraging some rural churches to move into town. In this instance, there was no Evangelical church in the town of Ortonville, and Conference leadership apparently saw this as a possible opportunity for expansion that might attract new members more readily than the rural and village churches in the area. Expansion into Ortonville did not ever take place, however.

117

In reviewing some of the building projects and/or improvements of the late 1940s (or of any era) it should be made clear that building projects do not necessarily indicate that a church congregation was fulfilling its mission. For the most part it did indicate growth and a real caring and concern for fulfilling mission. But sometimes some churches became so enamored of their building projects that they forgot what they were all about, while others sometimes valued frugality so highly that their buildings (more often than not the parsonage), did not reflect well on the congregation. Then as now, churches and congregations were made up of human beings whose frailties sometimes interfered with or slowed up the churches' mission. This was reflected in the Conference Superintendents' Report of 1948, as follows: "Unless a church seeks to reach out and win others in a community with a true missionary and evangelistic zeal, it does not merit the name of a church."[17]

E.U.B.'s in Minnesota, 1950-1960

With the dawning of a new decade and in 1951 the official joining of the Evangelical and United Brethren conferences in Minnesota, Conference leadership felt compelled to continue and expand the denomination's missionary expansion projects in the state. Even though there had been setbacks in the Robbinsdale project (primarily due to unexpected community opposition to location) this and the Richfield project proceeded, and there were plans for additional projects. As the Conference Superintendents' Report of 1950 stated:

Some of our families are living in other suburban areas of our state, some of which are developing at an unbelievable rate. Urgent requests have come to the Director of Missions that our Conference step in to serve...As a Conference we are limited to respond to such appeals to serve in growing communities because of lack of dedicated material resources.[18]

During the 1950s, the Minnesota Conference continued to work very hard to establish new mission churches. The first project begun in Robbinsdale (Olivet) in 1948, overcame many setbacks and grew rapidly. For example, membership in 1954 was 84 and had gone up to 131 by 1955. In 1960, this church was strengthened by the addition of many members from North Minneapolis' Hope Church which closed and united with Robbinsdale Olivet.

The Richfield Mission started officially in 1955 also was successful. This church - Richfield Church of Peace - had a membership of 112 in 1959 which had increased to 171 by 1960. The other suburban mission churches of the 1950s were both officially launched in 1958. These were to be located in Rochester and a suburb of St. Paul, Inver Grove Heights.

The printed page cannot adequately reflect or express the meaning these mission churches had for the Minnesota Conference. They bespoke years of hard work, dedication and sacrifice spent raising money, dealing with and overcoming setbacks and opposition and eventually succeeding in the establishment of new witnesses for the Evangelical United Brethren understanding of the Christian faith. Establishing these new churches was in a very real sense a leap of faith, and turning toward the new suburbs as a mission field must sometimes have seemed just as daunting as moving westward on the prairies had seemed to the Evangelical circuit-riders one hundred years earlier.

Ministerial Supply

With missionary expansion projects added to keeping all the other established churches functioning, the issue of adequate ministerial supply was very important. In 1954, Conference leadership professed a "...deep concern as to our future supply of ministers."[19] They noted that there was a 17.2 percent decrease in seminary enrollments nationwide; this decrease was not nearly as large in E.U.B. seminaries, however.[20] By 1957, the Conference Superintendents' Report indicated that this issue was becoming more crucial, and they expressed concern about how long the Minnesota Conference could maintain their traditional record of never having a vacant pulpit. They felt it might be necessary to have "yoked" churches with other denominations, more lay leadership, and small churches uniting with larger ones.

While there was the issue of declining seminary enrollment, there was also concern over ministers leaving the Minnesota Conference. Sometimes they left for another E.U.B. Conference, but more often than not they went to another denomination. Sometimes they left for theological reasons and occasionally the motivation was dissatisfaction with the episcopal system of appointment of ministers. These ministers usually became Presbyterians, where the call system (where individual churches hire their own minister) was in effect. And there may have been some whose motivation was a desire to get a larger congregation more quickly, or to join a denomination with higher salaries and better pension plans.

In trying to address these concerns, the Conference system of appointment had been made more humane and democratic than it was in the early days, with ministers now having more input into where they might be appointed. However, one of the core tenets of the episcopal system was that appointment served both congregations and ministers better than did the call system, in that the aim was to provide what a congregation needed more than what they might want. This meant, of course, that occasionally ministers and/or congregations were mildly or mightily displeased at what the appointment system brought them.

The other issues here, concerning more opportunities for movement within the system, higher salaries and better pension plans, were not insignificant, and Conference leadership certainly did recognize the need for improvement in these areas. There was no "quick fix" available, however, and some good, young ministers were lost to the E.U.B's in these post war years. It should be noted that this had occurred occasionally in earlier years as well, and there were ministers from other denominations or other E.U.B. conferences who throughout the years transferred into the Minnesota Conference.

One final item of note here is that in all of the lamentations about the declining numbers of men choosing the ministry not one word was spoken about the possibility of women being called to pastoral ministry. Old cultural and religious traditions do die hard, and though the Minnesota Conference was progressive in looking to the new suburban areas for expansion, it was not yet ready to speak on behalf of women ministers.

Cooperation With Other Denominations

During these post-war years Minnesota E.U.B.'s were also involved in cooperative ventures with other denominations. Cooperation was a necessity in getting the missionary expansion projects going in the new suburban areas, since location requests for new churches had to be approved by the Minneapolis Church Federation. There was also movement toward more cooperation with other denominations in areas of declining populations in rural areas such as southwest Minnesota.

It was felt that working toward yoked fields and/or merged churches in some of these areas would help free up resources needed for missionary expansion. These ideas were not necessarily received with enthusiasm by congregations in these rural areas who perhaps felt threatened by what they perceived to be a loss of identity. Conference leadership sought to be cognizant and understanding of these concerns, but also showed some impatience with those who feared change. The Conference Superintendents' Report of 1957 clearly expressed this, stating:

> Too often we see our mission as that of holding services, of perpetuating a church as a tribute to our fathers or of belonging to an exclusive fellowship group which we choose to call a church. These and many other similar conceptions of the Church are not adequate to stand the test of these days. ...Faithfulness to some people means doing the same things in the same way that we did them a generation

ago. Such faithfulness need not make much of a demand upon us. We need a willingness in our churches to face new adventures in the things of the spirit! We need the courage and faithfulness to try the thing that has not been tried and to do the thing that has not been done.[21]

While the above assessment may seem harsh, it is also very clear that the leadership of the Minnesota Conference was committed to moving the E.U.B Church forward and was not about to be content with the status quo. And while some may not have agreed with the direction of movement, the Conference leadership cannot be faulted for a lack of honesty and forthrightness in their stated goals. They believed that they had been elected to lead as well as serve, and they took their charge seriously.

Increased cooperation with other denominations was certainly a sign of the times, and other evidences of more ecumenical thinking were also present. In 1955, a Conference committee to explore ecumenical cooperation was formed, and specifically pointed out how historically, doctrinally and structurally, the E.U.B.'s were akin to the Methodists. This group also encouraged increased cooperation with evangelical denominations in local communities.[22] There was no real push for any immediate specific action on this, however, since the E.U.B. merger had just taken place in 1946, and the Minnesota Evangelical and United Brethren conferences had only formally united in 1951.

Lake Koronis Assembly Grounds

As the last chapter made clear, the purchase and development of the Lake Koronis Assembly Grounds was very important to the Minnesota Conference. The subsequent programs offered there quickly became a focal point for Minnesota Evangelicals and then E.U.B.'s after 1946/1951. Koronis was a unifying center for spiritual growth and Christian fellowship for those, clergy and lay persons alike, who participated in programs there.

This continued in the post-World War II years, and programs at Koronis continued to expand. The cabin camping program became a reality in 1952, with four cabins and a central lodge built on a sixty-five acre tract next to the Assembly Grounds. Camps were held here for children in grades four, five and six, and also for those in grades seven, eight and nine.[23] High school youth and adults continued to attend Assembly in June, and many other programs for lay people and clergy were conducted.

Evangelism and Social Action

The post-war years and especially the 1950s are now often thought of as years of tranquility and prosperity, particularly when compared to the turbulent 1960s. However, the 1950s were the years of the Korean War, the McCarthy anti-communist hysteria, an escalating "Cold War" with the Soviet Union, and the fear of nuclear war.

During this era there was a pronounced revival of interest in organized religion, and church membership in most denominations grew rapidly. The E.U.B. leadership expressed support for this renewed fervor, and the 1952 Conference Superintendents' Report stated:

> We are standing on the threshold of a revival in the Christian Church. Many communions are now stressing a warm and fervent evangelistic note in a way that they have never done before. We as an E.U.B. Church, because of our origin and heritage, should give enthusiastic support to this emphasis upon evangelism.[24]

There was, in the 1950s, a continued emphasis for Minnesota E.U.B.'s to "...recover the evangelistic fervor and passion of our fathers."[25] At the same time however, there was some concern voiced about "...the quality and depth of the current religious revival,"[26] on a national level. A real effort was made to distinguish between shallow and self-serving so-called evangelism and the evangelism which called people to take up their cross rather than to expect a life of ease.

The kind of evangelism the E.U.B.'s were propounding led very naturally to Christian social action. And while social concerns and action had always been important to Evangelicals/E.U.B.'s, they took on new urgency in the 1950s. The church was involved in such post-war efforts as CROP, the settlement of displaced persons from war-torn Europe, and the Heifer Project. And while they continued to address issues such as smoking, drinking, gambling and social dancing, there was a definite increased emphasis on the issue of race relations.

Historically the Evangelical/E.U.B Church had opposed slavery, but it remained a church whose members were of primarily German and other European backgrounds. But by the 1950s the leadership saw a need to address racial issues, and to reach out to other racial groups. They began a program of interracial vacation visits whereby black children from the Twin Cities spent a week at an E.U.B. farm home.

The Christian Social Action Committee that same year urged E.U.B.'s to keep their churches open to all people and opposed all forms of racial segregation. The Board of Missions reinforced this ideal, while at the same time stating that they were "...aware of the complicated sociological and economic factors which often make the ideal either difficult or impossible of accomplishment. This calls for leadership by idealists who are still capable of sound judgement."[27]

What stands out with great clarity in the reports on Minnesota E.U.B.'s in the 1950s is the emphasis on both evangelism/personal salvation and social action. The Conference Superintendents' Report of 1958 addresses this most eloquently, stating:

> We may be content to preach a "simple gospel" with a limited approach that encompasses only the individual - or we can propose to challenge our people with a concept of the Christian Gospel that embraces both individual salvation and social redemption. ..It is sheer hypocrisy for the Church to say that it cares for personality as sacred, and then to do nothing about collective evils that impinge on personality with frightful consequences.
>
> The Gospel – if rightly understood – is a rebuke to those who desire their smug complacency to be left undisturbed. An urgent need of our day is that the Church shall give a clear and courageous witness relating to crucial issues in the area of human relations.

Our Christian Gospel is relevant to the day in which we live. We must have a strong commitment to evangelism - but we must have a similar passion to proclaim the social implications of our Gospel to the day in which we live.[28]

This combined emphasis – evangelism and social action – made the E.U.B. Church quite unique for its time and for any time, including the present. It is not easy to balance the two, and it is a credit to E.U.B. leadership that they persisted in trying to do so.

The Prairie Churches in the 1950s

The 1950s were very active and exciting years for the churches in the three areas studied. These were quite prosperous years for farmers, and all three of these areas depended largely on agriculture. This prosperity was reflected not only in building projects, but in expanded activities and often growing memberships.

In south central Minnesota the winds of change were blowing in the 1950s, as two of Faribault County's six E.U.B. churches closed and united with the larger church on the same charge. Dunbar Zion closed in 1954 and united with Wells Salem, while Brush Creek Tabor closed in 1957 and united with Rice Lake Emmanuel which had remodeled its building in 1951. The Brush Creek Church had always been small; there were 31 members the year it closed.

Dunbar Zion was a different story, both because it was a much larger rural church – it had 104 members the year it closed – and because they had planned to build a new church themselves. Their building plans in the late 1940s had been postponed because of high building costs in the early post-war years. Then, by the early 1950s sentiment was shifting toward uniting with Wells. Some of the younger families felt that a larger congregation provided more programs for their children and young people, while others felt that they would lose the sense of closeness and family they had at Dunbar if they united with Wells. With hindsight they both may have been right, which is why these issues of church closure were sometimes very difficult for all concerned. Certainly by this time Conference leadership was inclined toward the closure of rural churches which could unite with a larger church, feeling that larger, more centrally located churches could offer more to their own people and to the general community. The Dunbar Zion Church did then vote to unite with Wells Salem, but not without some members feeling that they had been pressured into voting for the merger. In spite of some hard feelings, however, almost all of the Dunbar members transferred their membership to Wells, and in 1957 a new, larger church was erected in Wells.

There were some changes in southwestern Minnesota E.U.B. churches in the 1950s also. Marshall Salem built a new church in 1954, the rural Clifton congregation having united with them in 1947. Luverne Ebenezer relocated in town with both a new parsonage (1948) and a new church building in 1955. Here also there had been some reluctance on the part of some to move into town, even though it was not a matter of uniting with a larger congregation. There was also a new Pipestone Zion Church constructed in 1960.

There were no new churches built in western Minnesota in the 1950s but no churches were closed either. There continued

128

Church Membership: South Central Minnesota

Church	1940	1950	1960
Blue Earth Immanuel	120	159	183
Blue Earth Salem	408	470	496
Rice Lake Emmanuel	159	172	163
Brush Creek Tabor	30	32	Closed 1957
Wells Salem	156	231	339
Dunbar Zion	108	116	Closed 1954
Totals	981	1180	1181

Church Membership: Southwest Minnesota

Church	1940	1950	1960
Fairmont Salem	100	126	112
Welcome Emmanuel	71	83	58
Worthington Emmanuel	146	195	195
Luverne Ebenezer	61	56	29
Steen Salem	60	46	38
Pipestone Salem	82	71	72
Pipestone Zion	92	141	143
Hendricks Zion	71	117	141
Marshall Salem	104	198	231
Clifton Bethel	48	Closed 1947	–
Totals	835	1033	1019

Church Membership: Western Minnesota

Church	1940	1950	1960
Madison Ebenezer	51	87	117
Bellingham Zion	180	178	151
Yellowbank Emmanuel	61	65	56
Odessa Salem	110	83	68
Fairfield Zion	27	Closed 1940	–
Totals	429	413	392
GRAND TOTALS	**2245**	**2626**	**2592**

to be a decline in population in this part of Minnesota, and church membership continued to decline here for the most part. In spite of this, however, churches in this area made improvements to their buildings and the Yellowbank camp meetings held each year in June continued with good attendance throughout the 1950s. In fact, a new tabernacle building was erected on the Yellowbank Campgrounds in 1959, replacing the large tent.

Summary: 1946-1960

Clearly, these post-World War II years were years of change and challenge for the Evangelical/E.U.B. Church in Minnesota. The 1946 national merger between the Evangelical Church and the United Brethren in Christ, resulting in the new Evangelical United Brethren Church, was a major accomplishment and portent of things to come. This merger did not cause any major problems in Minnesota, where the two Conferences officially united in 1951. The Evangelicals in Minnesota had far outnumbered the United Brethren, and it is interesting to note that some of the old Evangelical churches had to be reminded to publicly acknowledge the merger. In both 1948 and 1949 the Conference admonished churches who were still using "Evangelical" and not "E.U.B." in their publicity and on bulletin boards, and urged all churches to use the new and correct title by July 1949.

The major challenge facing the new E.U.B. Church in Minnesota was how to confront and deal with the continued and accelerated population shift into the cities from rural areas. This was obviously an issue for all denominations, but it was a crucial issue for the E.U.B.'s both because they were a small denomination with more limited resources and because they had been historically overwhelmingly a small town and rural church. Church leadership had already begun to consider these issues before World War II, and the post-war years saw decisive and concerted action to begin and maintain new churches as missionary expansion projects in the growing suburbs. These efforts were continued and expanded in spite of setbacks, and in the face of continually needing to ask for more financial support of these projects from Minnesota E.U.B.'s. As was discussed earlier in this chapter, urban/rural issues had been increasing in importance. Clearly in these early post-war years, the E.U.B Church in Minnesota made a distinct turn toward the urban areas as the future of the church, but at the same time maintained a commitment to their small town and rural churches which still predominated.

In many ways this urban/rural issue can be compared to the German/English language issue which had confronted the Evangelical Association at the turn of the century. But where the language issue had finally boiled down to being "either/or," the urban/rural issue was more complex and not nearly as clearly defined. It was not an "either/or" issue, but rather a "both/and" issue and thus the real challenge was to strike a balance where the past, present and future could all be adequately served. Conflicts came between those who preferred to look to the past for guidance and those who chose to look to change to serve the future, but as in most human undertakings, both groups had legitimate concerns and hopes. At the time, the issues here were certainly not seen as insurmountable but rather as a challenge that should and could be met. This is seen clearly in the reports of the

Conference Superintendents during these years, as shown in this quote from the 1951 report:

> As a denomination, we have come to see that we have a responsibility for both the Rural and the Urban Church It is not a matter of "either-or"; it must be "both-and." We cannot be a strong Conference here in Minnesota if we have strong rural churches and weak city churches; nor can we be effective if we have strong city churches and weak, struggling rural churches. We must strengthen both areas of our work. City churches must have a concern for our rural work; for many families in our city churches have come from rural communities. And rural churches must likewise have a concern that city churches carry on effective work, for many young people go from our rural communities to city communities. All of us together are members of the E.U.B. Church; some of us live in the country and others of us live in the city. We stand together - or we fall together. "We are members one of another."[29]

The E.U.B.'s in Minnesota - lay people and clergy alike - were challenged to both preserve the past and launch new beginnings in the late 1940s and 1950s. They would be asked to continue to meet these challenges and new ones as well in the tumultuous 1960s, a decade that would see the merger of the E.U.B. Church with the Methodist Church in the new United Methodist Church.

Notes

[1] Behney and Eller, *The History of the EUB Church*, p. 279

[2] C.O. Main, "Historical Supplement, Minnesota Conference, Church of the United Brethren in Christ," *Minnesota Conference (UB) Official Record–1951* (Minneapolis, 1951), p. 19.

[3] Eller, *These EUB's*, p. 110.

[4] Behney and Eller, *The History of the EUB Church*, p. 281.

[5] Ibid., p. 357.

[6] Statistics, *Minnesota Conference (EV) Official Record–1951* (Harrisburg, 1951), pp. 40 and 52.

[7] Statistics, *Minnesota Conference (UB) Official Record–1951*, p. 37.

[8] *Ibid.*

[9] E.G. Moede, Report of the Board of Missions, *Minnesota Conference Official Record–1947* (Harrisburg, 1947), p. 123.

[10] *Ibid.*

[11] E. G. Moede and F. A. Spong, Report of the Conference Superintendents, *Minnesota Conference Official Record–1949* (Harrisburg, 1949), p. 51.

[12] D.C. Trapp, Report of the Director of Stewardship, *Minnesota Conference Official Record–1948* (Harrisburg, 1948) p. 129.

[13] Statistics, *Minnesota Conference Official Record–1947*, p. 80.

[14] Report of the Conference Administrative Council, *Minnesota Conference Official Record–1946* (Harrisburg, 1946), p. 49.

[15] *Ibid.*

[16] U.S. Department of Commerce, Bureau of the Census, *Sixteenth Census of the United States, 1940: Population.*

[17] E.G. Moede, F.A. Spong and D. C. Trapp, Report of the Conference Superintendents, *Minnesota Conference Official Record–1948* (Harrisburg, 1948), p. 42.

[18] F.A. Spong and E. G. Moede, Report of the Conference Superintendents, *Minnesota Conference Official Record–1950* (Harrisburg, 1950), p. 50.

[19] C.O. Main, F. A. Spong and H. E. Hiller, Report of the Conference Superintendents, *Minnesota Conference Official Record–1954* (Harrisburg, 1954), p. 53.

[20] *Ibid.*

[21] C.O. Main, F. A. Spong and H. E. Hiller, Report of the Conference Superintendents, *Minnesota Conference Official Record–1957* (Harrisburg, 1957), p. 68.

[22] W.W. Zahl, Report of the Committee on Christian Social Action, *Minnesota Conference Official Record–1955* (Harrisburg, 1955), p. 95.

[23] R.S. Heitke, "The First Eight Years Together" (Minneapolis, 1959), p. 8

[24] C.O. Main, H. E. Hiller and F. A. Spong, Report of the Conference Superintendents, *Minnesota Conference Official Record–1952* (Harrisburg, 1952), p. 55.

[25] C.O. Main, H. E. Hiller and F. A. Spong, Report of the Conference Superintendents, *Minnesota Conference Official Record–1955* (Harrisburg, 1955), p. 58.

[26] *Ibid.*

[27] F.A. Spong, Proceedings of Board of Missions, *Minnesota Conference Official Record–1957* (Harrisburg, 1957), p. 135.

[28] C.O. Main, H. E. Hiller, F. A. Spong, Report of the Conference Superintendents, *Minnesota Conference Official Record–1958* (Harrisburg, 1958), p. 66.

[29] F.A. Spong, Report of the Director of Missions, *Minnesota Conference (Ev) Official Record–1951* (Harrisburg, 1951), p. 73.

Chapter Seven

Merging Into Mainstream Methodism:
1961 – 1968

The Turbulent Sixties

In looking back at past eras it is easy to over-simplify and/or generalize. When we look at and compare the 1950s and 1960s, for example, the 1950s may bring to mind an era of benign prosperity, while the 1960s may conjure up a time of chaos and confusion. There may indeed be some truth in the above statements but they are generalizations and they are dependent on the lenses through which one looks back on past decades.

The seeds of the 1960s were sown in the 1950s and in the earlier decades of the Great Depression and World War II. The desire for a return to "normalcy" (a subjective word if there ever was one!) was very powerful in the 1950s, resulting in some much needed stability for many, and in continued discrimination for others. The civil rights movement led by Dr. Martin Luther King and others began in the South in the 1950s, and became a national crusade in the 1960s, resulting in legislation to help protect minority rights.

Other movements and causes also came to the fore in the 1960s including the anti-Viet Nam war and women's movements and youth movements which included the sexual revolution and the drug/hippie culture. And while these disparate movements all occurred in the 1960s and continued into the 1970s it is perilous to lump them all together since they each had different methods and goals. Their one common denominator was an espousal of change and rebellion from the status quo, and this, along with the violence sometimes engendered by change often polarized different segments of society.

Issues Facing the Christian Church in the 1960s

The church, through its different denominations, was challenged to respond to the many rapidly occurring changes of the 1960s. Some denominations, including the E.U.B.'s, were supportive of the non-violent civil rights movement and became increasingly critical of the U.S. involvement in Viet Nam. Taking positions on the various youth movements was more fraught with peril, and required serious examination of core Christian values in a rapidly changing society.

Along with the major issues of the 1960s, most denominations faced declining memberships and fewer candidates for the parish ministry. The E.U.B.'s were not immune to these problems, and in addition, the rural to urban population shift continued to affect them. Both the Evangelical and the United Brethren Churches had historically been largely located in rural areas or small towns, and after the 1946 merger, the E.U.B.'s as a united church began to feel the effects of the post-World War II movement from rural areas to the cities and their suburbs. Certainly they had some city churches (particularly in the eastern United States), but not in comparable numbers to other denominations.

E.U.B Movement Toward Union/Merger, 1958-1964

The E.U.B. leadership on a national level sought to find solutions to the problems they faced in the post-war 1940s and 1950s. By the mid-1950s there was some feeling that the E.U.B.'s would be well advised to seek to unite with another similar denomination. Reasons given for pursuing union were both that a more united and ecumenical witness was right and necessary, and that in an age of increasing costs and diminishing resources it would prevent duplication and put scarce resources to better use.

In reporting on the October 1958 General Conference of the E.U.B. Church, the E.U.B. weekly *The Telescope Messenger* of November 8, 1958 stated that interest in union was expressed toward the Church of the Brethren, the Churches of God, and especially the Methodist Church. A minority report, more hesitant toward union exploration with the Methodists, was also offered. The final compromise recommendation was:

> ...to further study and explore the possible advantages and the potential problems involved in organic union with the Methodist Church and to report thereon from time to time

139

through the church press and in such other manner as it may deem advisable...to continue exploratory conversations with the Commission on Church Union of the Methodist Church for the purpose of developing possible bases of consideration for union.[1]

Prior to this there had been some discussion of union in *The Telescope Messenger*, such as Reverend W. Cecil Findley's article in April 1958, which advocated union with the Methodists.[2] Lively discussion ensued in letters to *The Telescope Messenger*, with responses ranging from disapproval to delight. Articles continued to appear in *The Telescope Messenger*. They ranged from "The Methodists Speak to Evangelical United Brethren" by Bishop Ensley of the Methodist Church in support of union,[3] to Reverend Kenneth Krueger's "Is There a Future for the Evangelical United Brethren Church?" which called for a spiritual reawakening within the E.U.B. Church as a first priority.[4]

No further mention was made of union overtures to either The Church of the Brethren or Churches of God: it is interesting that neither of these churches felt compelled to pursue union with a similar and/or larger denomination. There were some consultations (the Blake-Pike proposal, named for Dr. Eugene Carson Blake, Stated Clerk of the United Presbyterian Church, USA, and James A. Pike, Episcopalian Bishop), regarding a major church union of the United Presbyterian Church, the Protestant Episcopal Church, the Methodist Church, the United Church of Christ, and later the Disciples of Christ, the E.U.B.'s, and the Polish National Church.[5] This mega-union proposal, or Consultation on Church Union (COCU), was seriously considered for a number of years, but did not come to fruition because of numerous difficulties and differences.

Talks between the Methodists and E.U.B.'s, however, accelerated in the early 1960s, and articles and letters in *The Telescope Messenger* reflected this. A major two-part article appeared shortly before the October 1962 E.U.B. General Conference, titled "Shall General Conference Authorize a Basis of Union with the Methodists?"[6] The "Yes" response was given by Dr. G. Weir Hartman, a member of the E.U.B. Ohio East Conference and Executive Director of the Columbus Area Council of Churches, and put forth several reasons for union. He maintained that "Union is not a comfortable option. It is a necessity. Under the trends of present social and political movements, it is a matter of survival." He felt strongly that union was a "...step in the direction of Christ's will for his Church," and that E.U.B.'s, while giving up something, would "...gain far more than we can possibly give."[7]

The "No" response was given by John K. Bergland, Pastor of Beavertown E.U.B. Church at Kettering in the Ohio-Miami Conference. He felt first, that, "...if any merger is to have a firm foundation, it must develop from free opportunity and equal expression in the framework of a democratic process." He maintained that too many of those supporting Union were "...willing, indeed anxious, to worship at the altars of the gods of bigness, success and recognition," and that it was dangerous to "...use merger as a substitute for mission." He was convinced that the merger being suggested was a merger without meaning, and concluded: "It is not enough to point to our cherished heritages and say that these insure the meaning of this merger. We must this day be open to the leading of the Holy Spirit, looking for the revitalization of Christian doctrine and the re-birth of warm-hearted evangelism."[8]

There were wide, varied, and thoughtful responses to these views on union with the Methodists, ranging from total opposition to total support, and many views in-between these extremes. The 1962 General Conference of the E.U.B. Church met in October 1962, and these views were reflected in the deliberations. This 1962 General Conference voted to authorize the Commission on Union to proceed in working on a basis of union with the Methodist Church. The vote was 310 affirmative to 94 negative. Considering that this vote was simply to proceed with union discussions, it was certainly not an unqualified mandate supporting union; it reflected much ambivalence.

Union discussions proceeded, and the February 1963 issue of *The Telescope Messenger* included a statement by Paul A. Washburn, who was then Chairman of the Reporting Committee on Union. He pointed out that the Commission on Union first had to come up with an actual plan which then had to be approved by the Commission itself, then by a future session of the General Conference, and finally by the annual conferences. Washburn also stressed that the term "union" rather than "merger" should be used. He stated, "Merger is a process of one entity being swallowed up by another. A union is a process of forming a new entity in which all the interests of the uniting bodies are conserved in a new entity."[9] This distinction between "union" and "merger" would not soon disappear, however, since many

E.U.B.'s felt that their being outnumbered about fourteen to one would result in a merger, not a union, no matter what it was officially called.

A joint session of the E.U.B. and Methodist executive committees was held in late 1962 and formed the Joint Commission on Church Union. Their meeting in March 1963 called for a statement of principles for a plan and basis of union to be presented to the General Conference of the Methodist Church in April 1964; approval of this statement by a two-thirds majority would lead to a complete plan and basis of union to be submitted to the E.U.B. General Conference in October 1966. If approved by a three-fourths majority this would then be submitted to the annual conferences of both denominations. Then it would come before the 1968 Methodist General Conference with a possibility that "...a specially called session of the E.U.B. General Conference at the time of the 1968 Methodist General Conference could become the 'Uniting Conference' for the two denominations."[10]

Some cogent comments by *The Telescope Messenger* editor Joe Willard Krecker are illustrative of the discussions going on primarily within the leadership of the E.U.B. Church, as most local congregations and even conferences were not yet heavily involved with the issue. Krecker's editorial of March 30, 1963, states: "It is not necessary that Evangelical United Brethren stumble hastily to lose our denominational identity." He then suggests that the Commission on Union be given "...complete and prayerful support as they work on a possibility of a basis of union," and that "...the result ought to be a real revival of what Methodism was in the beginning - and Evangelical United Brethrenism, as well."[11]

The Methodist General Conference of April 1964 did indeed approve the Statement of Principles for a Plan and Basis of Union, and the stage was now set for the E.U.B.'s to proceed with their own discussions of union before their General Conference of October 1966. Union discussions then accelerated in 1964 with meetings of the Joint Commission on Union and interpretations given of these meetings.

Church and Home (formerly *The Telescope Messenger*) editor J.W. Krecker stated that "Contrary to doubts and fears expressed by some, this joint commission on union is not a pressure group. No one is being 'pushed' into a union."[12] On the other hand, there were letters to *Church and Home* disputing this view, such as one asking:

> Is it democratic when the desire for union comes not from the people but from the upper echelons of administrative officials of the Church? ...Is it democratic when all well-organized agencies of the Church for preparation and promotion are used to support the proposed union while the opposition is practically limited to the means that I am now using in 'letters'?[13]

Letters, articles and editorials also addressed specific union issues such as the name of the "new" church, the election and tenure of bishops, the election or appointment of conference superintendents, and theological and social issues of importance to clergy and laity alike. These union/merger issues on both the national and state level as they developed in the years 1965-1968 will be discussed further at the end of this chapter.

Minnesota E.U.B.'s in the 1960s

At the state level, at least in Minnesota, there did not seem to be much discussion of a specific or possibly imminent union or merger with the Methodist Church until about 1964. It was in 1964 that the Methodist General Conference voted to proceed with union negotiations with the E.U.B.'s. when Bishop Heininger presented information on the proposed union to the 1964 Minnesota Annual Conference, and a discussion and question period followed. The bishop asked that reactions to the proposed basis of union be relayed to him in writing for submittal to the Commission on Union.[14] The next step was for the E.U.B.'s to vote on this union plan at their own General Conference in 1966. Between 1964 and 1966, then, the proposed union was a major topic of discussion for many Minnesota E.U.B.'s; this discussion will be detailed further on in this chapter.

New Mission Churches in the 1960s

The major issues for Minnesota E.U.B.'s in the early 1960s continued to revolve around the rural to urban population shift, which was resulting in fewer opportunities for growth in rural areas and the need to continue to begin new mission churches in the growing urban areas.

The three mission churches established between 1949 and 1958 (Robbinsdale Olivet, Richfield Church of Peace, and Rochester Bethany) were joined in 1960 by Inver Grove Heights Mount Bethel. Long-range planning by the Conference called for four new mission churches in the metropolitan area by 1968. This was a very ambitious and optimistic plan, but was not thought to be unrealistic. The mission churches already established were succeeding; for example, in 1962 it was reported that the three latest ones (Peace, Bethany, and Mount Bethel) showed a gain of 211 members (excluding E.U.B. transfers) in the previous four years, while the net gain for the entire Conference was only 129 in this four-year period.[15] The next six years did indeed see the establishment of four new mission churches: Lake Elmo Hope in 1962, Burnsville River Hills in 1964, Plymouth Pilgrim in 1966 and Bloomington Normandale Hylands in 1968.

Ministerial Supply Problems

The 1960s saw a real decrease in those entering the ministry in general, and particularly the pastoral ministry. This was true in most denominations across the country including the E.U.B.'s in Minnesota. As the 1962 Conference Superintendents' Report stated:

> Living in an atmosphere of specialization, which glamorizes the dramatic, many of our candidates find themselves lured to other fields of Christian service by the time they have completed their seminary training. [The call to pastoral ministry] is a call to a superhuman task, possible only by the miracle of God's grace. Here you deal with all of life, every age, all of man's problems, joys and sorrows, successes and failures, material and mental, social and spiritual needs. All professions combined cannot answer for what the pastor is called to do.[16]

Along with stressing the importance of the parish ministry, the report also points out that congregations all too often made it difficult for parish ministers to retain enthusiasm for their calling. Their exasperation with this kind of congregation clearly shows here when they say:

If you laymen want a 'go-getter' minister then you should not throw a block on the track every time he wants to help you move ahead. Release the brakes, use the 'tools' he suggests, or you may be the cause of driving him out of the work, or surely away from your church.[17]

The issue of dwindling numbers of parish ministers comes up repeatedly in the 1960s. The same themes discussed above - why ministers were not choosing the parish ministry, and how congregations sometimes made real ministry most difficult for their ministers - were clearly of grave importance to Minnesota's E.U.B. leadership. Attempting to deal with this issue and with the implications of the continuing decline in population in rural areas brought change and innovation in many areas. New cooperative arrangements - yoking of congregations and/or mergers with Methodist congregations in some areas - took place. Some were successful, others were not; some were truly supported by local churches while others barely got lukewarm support. But all of these efforts were put forth to continue the E.U.B. Church's mission in Minnesota in a time of change and turmoil.

Small Town and Rural Church Issues in the 1960s

Issues facing small town and rural E.U.B. churches in Minnesota in the 1960s were closely intertwined with those of ministerial supply, and the new missions to serve the growing suburban population. One of the ways Conference tried to address the issue of diminishing resources was by a cooperative venture with the Methodists to "yoke" fields. In a yoked field, a small Methodist and a small E.U.B. church in a small town or rural area would be served by the same minister and share resources. These were not mergers, but rather a sharing of resources.

In 1961, yoked fields were created in three areas involving three E.U.B. churches (Pleasant Prairie, Eyota, and Hendricks) with nearby Methodist churches. These were each to be served by an E.U.B. minister, with no attempt to unite the two churches in each area. Yoking churches in areas where it was difficult to maintain a small church alone seemed to be both practical and a manifestation of the current ecumenicity. This is reflected in the 1961 Conference Superintendents' Report which decries the "...scandalous overlapping of pastoral energies and the sinful competition that often exists between small churches of denominations with similar emphasis in close geographic proximity and especially in small towns."[18]

Conference leadership continued to stress the necessity for small churches to reach out in new ways in order to assure their own existence and more importantly, to fulfill their mission as a church. The 1962 Conference Superintendents' Report castigates churches whose mission appeared to be "...to maintain an organization for a family group or for the sake of glorious tradition - one whose future is all in the past." Churches with declining memberships where there seemed to be no real hope for growth were urged to "...seek continuation of life by merger or yoking with another."[19]

The Conference Superintendents continued to express their concerns and to respond to accusations that they were trying to close up churches or kill congregations. Clearly there were some feelings of animosity toward Conference in congregations which were urged or forced (depending on one's point of view), into mergers of two E.U.B. churches or ventures with other denominations.

The Superintendents' Report of 1965 addresses these issues explicitly, stating in "The Anatomy of the Death of a Church":

> Our business is to open and strengthen churches. Occasionally, however, we are called upon to hold the 'last rites,' or provide the 'coup de grace' for, or have the 'committal service' over a church that is mortally wounded or has already expired. CHURCHES *NEVER* DIE BY CONFERENCE ACTION! They usually die by their own hand.[20]

Continuing, they give three major reasons for the death of a church: old age, arteriosclerosis, and egocentricity. To die of old age was seen as no disgrace, and was to:

> ...have lived a good life, made a significant contribution to the world, and have been a blessing to all. Death is due to the attrition of time and the simple migration of people from the area so that new-life potential is non-existent. The death of such a church should be triumphant! [21]

Surely a fair number of the churches which had closed in the Minnesota Conference had met this criteria, closing (or often merging with a nearby larger church) because there were too few families left in the area to warrant continuation.

The other two reasons for the death of a church – arteriosclerosis and egocentricity – were not so benign. Dying of arteriosclerosis included such factors as internal strife, an antagonistic spirit (being negative toward change or to anything different or from "outside"), faulty or inadequate stewardship, and passive programs. Dying of egocentricity meant being so self-centered and content with the status quo that any real sense of a larger mission was totally lost.[22]

The concerns expressed by Conference leadership in the 1960s were based on their observations as they interacted with churches large and small, all over Minnesota. Clearly they were becoming impatient with churches that they perceived as not making changes that would enhance these churches' mission in their own communities. Some new arrangements, such as yoked congregations, seemed imperative for survival. They were also concerned about all churches in the Conference making contributions for the new mission churches in the suburbs. They were looking at the "big picture," for the future of the Conference as a whole.

Individual churches, on the other hand, did not necessarily have the same priorities, and often tended quite naturally to be more concerned with their own congregations' particular issues than with larger Conference issues. This was even more pronounced in stressful times. People in areas of dwindling population, with young people leaving the area, often were worried about keeping their own land and farms and about the survival of their communities. The churches in these areas reflected these concerns, and were thus often not too likely to be too enthusiastic about contributing to mission churches in the suburbs.

Also, while merging with another E.U.B. church, yoking with another small church of a different denomination, or moving a country church into town might be eminently logical to Conference leadership, that did not mean these solutions would be welcomed with open arms by the churches themselves. Change was confronting these people on every side, and it is not surprising that they then often sought to keep their churches as a refuge from those stressful changes. The "big picture" was often just not as relevant to them as it was to Conference leadership. Financial support and other resources for struggling small town and rural congregations might well have been seen as more useful than new mission churches or mergers, yokings or moves for themselves.

Churches and their congregations varied widely in their responses to change and urgings of Conference leadership as to how to survive and thrive. Certainly there were churches who consistently resisted change of any kind and who clung to the past so tightly that the future (and even the present) were meaningless abstractions. Others sought to meet the challenge of changing times while still remaining true to their heritage and to their mission as Christian E.U.B. churches. And many were in-between, as they tried to deal with challenges brought by changing times.

As this chapter has made clear, the 1960s were years of turmoil and change, and the church generally and churches specifically were called upon to respond to deal with the times. This was true in the prairie churches as well.

South Central Minnesota E.U.B.'s in the 1960s

In south central Minnesota, the four remaining Evangelical/ E.U.B. churches in this study, (Blue Earth Immanuel, Blue Earth Salem, Rice Lake and Wells, did not experience major upheavals in the 1960s. The two smaller country churches had united with nearby E.U.B. churches in the 1950s; i.e., Dunbar Zion with Wells Salem in 1954 and Brush Creek Tabor with Rice Lake Emmanuel in 1957. The four churches were all now single charges (i.e., one church/one minister) and ranged in size from 163 to 496 in 1960 (see chart, p. 157 for all membership numbers). Membership in these four churches combined was 1,181 in 1960; this total had declined to 1,058 in 1967, reflecting both the general population decline in Faribault County and the declining church membership of the 1960s. While this membership decline is significant over time, it was certainly not a cause for panic. The cluster of E.U.B. churches in Faribault County, both in town and in the country, were holding their own in the 1960s.

Southwestern Minnesota E.U.B.'s in the 1960s

The situation was somewhat different in southwestern Minnesota, where the E.U.B churches were smaller and were scattered over six counties. In 1960 four of them (Luverne, Steen, Welcome and Pipestone Salem) had between 29 and 72 members, and while five of the nine were located in towns of some size, only one (Marshall Salem) had over 200 members. Numbers do not necessarily reflect success or failure, and many small congregations continued to do very well. Whether they could keep going in an area which was steadily losing population was a concern, however, and every church/congregation in southwest Minnesota as elsewhere, reacted and responded to the challenge of the times in their own way.

Pipestone Zion had built a new church in a new location in Pipestone in 1960, and membership actually increased between 1960 and 1967. The Conference-urged relocation of Luverne (Pleasant View) Ebenezer from the country into town in 1955, however, did not thrive; membership in 1955 was 38 and was 30 in 1966 when the church closed. Many from this congregation then transferred to the Steen Salem Church, served by the same minister.

Major changes were also occurring in the Hendricks (New Grove) Zion Church. This church, located near the South Dakota border, was the only E.U.B. church in Lincoln County. Since it was too far away from any other E.U.B. church to be regularly served as a joint charge, it had sometimes been difficult to station full-time ministers there. In spite of these difficulties, this church had grown steadily, and had a membership of 141 in 1960.

In 1961, one of three pilot projects of the Conference involved the Hendricks E.U.B. Church in a yoking arrangement with the Hendricks Methodist Church.[23] The combined congregation would have an E.U.B. minister and would, of course, share other resources. As is so often the case, there are no written records of the local congregation's views on this yoking; we can assume that the response was mixed. This yoked/combined congregation, in any case, came up with a Basis of Union, in which the new united church would be named Grace United (neither E.U.B. or Methodist) Church of Hendricks.[24] With national merger efforts coming to fruition the Hendricks union did not occur until after the national merger, when the two churches instead then became Grace United Methodist Church of Hendricks.

Other E.U.B. churches in southwest Minnesota saw some loss in membership in the 1960s, but perhaps not as great as might have been expected. The rural Welcome church's membership had started to decline in the 1950s, going from 75 in 1956 to 50 in 1967, but membership decline took place in some town churches also; Marshall Salem's membership dropped from 231 in 1960 to 193 in 1967.

It is important to remember as was noted earlier, that numbers do not always tell the whole story. Some small churches are able to provide a vital spiritual witness, while some large churches manage to maintain only a large building and inflated membership numbers. It is clear, however, that the "numbers game" became increasingly important in the 1960s as the E.U.B.'s and other denominations also faced shortages in parish ministers and the need to follow the population from small towns and rural areas to the city and suburbia. This was especially crucial for the E.U.B.'s, whose base had always been small towns and rural areas.

Western Minnesota E.U.B.'s in the 1960s

There were four churches (five counting the Correll church served with Bellingham) left in western Minnesota in 1960. The Bellingham and Madison churches were just holding their own, while decline in membership was more marked in the Odessa and Yellowbank churches. This decline continued and Conference urged these two churches to unite and use the Odessa village location. There was some opposition to this union, particularly from some of Yellowbank Emmanuel's members. These were primarily people whose forebears had built this church in 1881, the first Evangelical church in Lac Qui Parle County.

Standing as it did on a rise in open country with its cemetery beside it, this church could be seen for miles around. Within its walls marriages were performed, babies baptized, the Christian gospel proclaimed and received, prayers said in times of sickness or health, and of good and bad harvests, and finally the last rites for the dead who were then buried a few steps away. Perhaps it was time for the last rites to now be said for this church itself as had happened in 1931 with Salem and in 1940 with Fairfield Zion. This did not necessarily make it easy to accept at Yellowbank and many other places. It is sometimes hard for people to look to the future if they feel their past is being taken away from them.

The Odessa and Yellowbank congregations did unite in January 1963, forming the Hope E.U.B. Church. The Odessa church building was really too small for the joint congregation, and after much deliberation the Odessa building was sold and the larger Yellowbank building was moved to Odessa in 1965. The move into Odessa was a traumatic one, as the building twice fell off the flatbed truck on its way. There was some loss of old members in the newly formed Hope Church, as some former Yellowbank members transferred into the Bellingham Zion or Big Stone Tabor (across the border in South Dakota) E.U.B. churches instead. The two churches (Odessa and Yellowbank) had a combined membership of 124 in 1960 and the united Hope Church's membership was 77 in 1967.

Another major development in the late 1960s for the western Minnesota churches was the movement toward a cooperative parish in this area. This concept was first suggested by Methodist ministers in the area, Reverend Dwight Haberman of the Ortonville Methodist Church and Reverend Ted Colescott of the Clinton Methodist and Graceville United Church of Christ. E.U.B., Methodist, Presbyterian and United Church of Christ representatives were invited to meet and discuss the concept in February 1967. Progress was slow, but steady, and by mid-1968 a group of eleven congregations in the area were ready to proceed. Since the E.U.B./Methodist union took place in April 1968, the realization of this cooperative parish in western Minnesota will be discussed in the next chapter.

Merger Plans Accelerate

Merger/union discussions took center stage for the E.U.B.'s on a national level in the years 1965-1967. This issue had been prominent in the ten preceding years; it now became a predominant concern. This is not to say that E.U.B. leadership was solely involved with merger/union, as many moral and social concerns of the 1960s continued to confront the church as well. But many, if not most, of those in positions of national leadership of the E.U.B. Church felt that union with the Methodists was the highest priority, and concentrated on this goal.

There were others, however, who felt that E.U.B. national

Church Membership: South Central Minnesota

Church	1960	1961	1962	1963	1964	1965	1966	1967
Bl. Earth Imm.	183	175	181	177	175	158	155	151
Bl. Earth Salem	496	479	453	440	435	416	421	403
Rice Lake	163	166	159	158	162	159	157	154
Wells	339	342	340	337	327	332	341	350
Totals	1181	1162	1133	1112	1099	1065	1074	1058

Church Membership: Southwestern Minnesota

Church	1960	1961	1962	1963	1964	1965	1966	1967
Fairmont	112	105	106	109	112	110	105	104
Welcome	58	55	54	57	57	50	47	50
Worthington	195	193	185	181	177	187	185	192
Luverne	29	28	27	28	28	30	30	closed
Steen	38	40	40	45	45	47	47	61
Pipestone Salem	72	74	80	78	74	69	68	66
Pipestone Zion	143	150	152	150	156	142	147	153
Hendricks	141	143	131	129	131	133	135	135
Marshall	231	221	201	204	202	191	201	193
Totals	1019	1009	976	981	982	959	965	954

Church Membership: Western Minnesota

Church	1960	1961	1962	1963	1964	1965	1966	1967
Bellingham	151	146	157	154	163	160	152	147
Madison	117	118	125	120	118	121	118	113
Odessa Salem	68	72	71	67				
Yellowbank Em.	56	58	53	47				
Odessa Hope					94	90	83	77
Totals	392	394	406	388	375	371	353	337

Grand Totals	2592	2565	2515	2481	2456	2395	2392	2349

leaders should have been spending more of their time leading and caring for the E.U.B. Church and some maintain that had this occurred, the E.U.B. Church might well have entered a period of growth and renewal on its own, as did some of the other smaller denominations (see Chapter Nine, note #7). Obviously one cannot know what might have been, but it is a thought-provoking concept nonetheless.

Discussions of merger/union were spirited and heartfelt as reflected in *Church and Home* editorials, articles and letters in 1965-1967. Proponents of union stressed that it was wrong for Christ's church to be divided, using Biblical references to reinforce this position. Those who were not necessarily opposed to merger but were not yet convinced of its rightness, maintained that they were not sure that organic union was necessarily God's will. This group was generally committed to ecumenicity, but believed, as stated by a Methodist, Willard M. Mecklenburg, that "...interdenominational unity of purpose and action can be achieved without organic union."[25]

Another major issue was the size differential between Methodists and E.U.B.'s and the related questions of whether being bigger was in any or most ways better. Proponents of union maintained that while bigger was not per se better, being larger provided many more opportunities for the church's witness. Greater name recognition was also thought to be of value here. Others felt that bigness too often led to organization for its own sake and a loss of grass roots participation and involvement.

An article relating to the size issue appeared in *Church and Home* on September 1, 1966, entitled "Fourteen to One: The

Odds of Merger" by contributing editor Harvey M. Chinn. His essay dealt with the size disparity of E.U.B.'s to Methodists and his thesis that union was really merger, whereby the E.U.B. Church would join the Methodist Church, in "...an expanded version of Methodism, in which E.U.B. patterns are generally lost and absorbed."[26] C.R. Findley, Conference Superintendent of the Kansas Conference, wrote an accompanying rebuttal to Chinn's thesis, entitled "Fifteen Plus One: Opportunity for Renewal." Findley believed that there could be authentic union between E.U.B.'s and Methodists, stating: "People who are spiritually sensitive to each other and have respect for each other's traditions can work wonders in the spirit of Christian unity."[27]

Other issues brought up related to some E.U.B.'s concerns about Methodists being too "liberal." Many of these people felt that it was important to maintain their German pietistic and evangelistic heritage, and that this could/would be lost or diluted in union/merger. This was often genuine and heartfelt concern, but was sometimes a "holier-than-thou" attitude as well. There was also major concern about ecclesiastical structure. In the Methodist Church bishops were elected for life and conference superintendents appointed by the bishop, while the E.U.B.'s elected both bishops and conference superintendents for four year terms. The E.U.B. concern was that the Methodist structure was more autocratic and monarchial and less democratic than that of the E.U.B.'s.

In addition to the issues discussed above, there were also concerns expressed about not only "why" union was desirable, but also as to the "when" and "how." Proponents of union believed that if union was desirable then it made eminent sense to pursue this goal with all deliberate speed, while others felt that even if union was the desired end, there need be no undue haste or panic driving its consummation. There seems to have been a difference in perception here, with those who had been involved in union discussions since the late 1950s feeling that there had been ample time, while many laypeople, and clergy as well, often felt that the possibility of a union/merger had not really been made clear to them until 1964-1965, leaving them little time for reflection. Many felt that pressure was used to persuade those who viewed union with caution and reluctance.

A related issue here was that of dissemination of information on union talks with the general membership of the E.U.B. Church. There were inquiries from both clergy and laypeople about the lack of printed information or opportunities for discussion. As one layperson asked in 1965: "Why have we not had full, open, and honest discussions, with instructive and constructive pertinent information at hand in every local parish on this very debatable subject...?"[28] Another layperson wrote: "I am not nearly so opposed to merger with the Methodist Church as I am opposed to the procedures our Church has used thus far to bring it about. I believe that there must be some place for the 'grass roots,' the local church to voice its convictions."[29]

Those engaged in union discussions did attempt to meet this need for information by preparing and disseminating a booklet entitled "Our Churches Face Union," in 1966. *The Telescope Messenger* and then *Church and Home* had also attempted to bring union/merger issues to the fore for E.U.B.'s, particularly from 1964 to 1967.

Information on union/merger for Methodists was far less prevalent; *Together*, the Methodist equivalent of *Church and Home*, had about one-fourth the number of articles as did *Church and Home* pertaining to union between 1964-1967. Many of these articles were to inform Methodists about who the E.U.B.'s were, as it must be remembered that many Methodists, particularly in the South, had never met an E.U.B. face to face, and may never have heard of them before the 1960s.

There were also meetings held throughout the various conferences in 1965 and 1966; these were sometimes perceived as "too little, too late," and as somewhat condescending in nature, but they did attempt to provide necessary information to E.U.B.'s throughout the country. The directives given by the E.U.B. General Conference of 1962 were being carried out, but the ways in which this was done did not necessarily please everyone.

Minnesota E.U.B.'s and Union/Merger, 1964-1966

Information on the possibilities and plans of union/merger with the Methodists started appearing on a regular basis in the *Minnesota Conference News Review* (published bi-monthly) in 1964. Informational articles were presented as well as pro and con opinions by both clergy and laypeople. Many favored union on the basis of presenting a stronger witness in many Minnesota communities where both E.U.B.'s and Methodists were struggling. It was also pointed out that there were often problems related to current yokings/unions of small struggling churches. As Conference Superintendent E. R. Praetorius wrote:

Yokings and unions in Minnesota – except perhaps for one –
are not the result of any burning desire for brotherly love and
the expression of an ecumenical spirit, but of a pragmatic
need for sheer survival. This is not – in fact – a grass roots
move toward denominational union. [30]

Concerns were also expressed about the speed with which
negotiations were moving toward culmination, and taking more
time to bring union/merger about was suggested. These and
other concerns and needs were voiced in a Report of the Special
Committee on Church Union and Renewal to the Minnesota
E.U.B. Conference Council of Administration in July 1965. This
report stressed the need for more information stating: "It is evident that on the local church and conference levels there is a definite lack of understanding, vital interest and enthusiasm concerning Union." The report also pointed out the need to get better acquainted with Methodists, for adequate time to consider
union and for ecumenical commitment.[31]

On the whole, it would appear from the written record that
union/merger was generally favored, (albeit not enthusiastically
by some), by Conference leadership and many informed clergy
and laypeople. However, clearly there remained many clergy as
well as laypeople who felt they had not been given enough information to make an informed decision and who were lukewarm, at
best, toward union.

Merger Plans Become Reality

The E.U.B. General Conference met in Chicago in November
1966, with one of the major agenda items being the vote on the

Plan and Basis of Union with the Methodist Church. A three-fourths majority for union was required, and the vote as taken was 325 for and 88 against or 78.7 percent for union. Voting by secret ballot was not allowed and delegates were required to stand to register their vote. The specially-called General Conference of the Methodist Church, also meeting at Chicago, voted 90 percent for union.[32]

The next step to bring the union to fruition was the vote required in all of the annual conferences of both churches; a two-thirds majority of all annual conference members was required to adopt the Plan of Union.[33] The Minnesota Annual Conference voted 103 "yes," "32" no, with 2 abstentions, thus approving the Plan of Union by 76.3 percent.[34] Voting by all thirty-two annual conferences was to be completed by late 1967, and the two-thirds majority vote was reached. The Pacific Northwest and Montana Conferences voted to stay out of the union. The Uniting Conference had been scheduled in advance to take place in Dallas, Texas in April 1968.

The Uniting Conference then did take place as anticipated, creating what would now be known as the United Methodist Church. Ex-Methodists in the new church numbered 10,289,214 while ex-E.U.B.'s numbered 746,099.[35] This union (or merger, depending on one's point of view) meant different things to different people. Powerfully mixed feelings were experienced by many, and particularly those from the E.U.B. side. One view was expressed by Curtis Chambers, the editor of *Church and Home*, as he spoke of "...a renewing spirit of commitment in Christian mission by which former Methodists and Evangelical United

Brethren were welded together to create a present and future fellowship."[36]   Another perspective was offered by Joe Willard Krecker, former editor of *Church and Home*, who stated:

> To suppose that The United Methodist Church is a 'new' Church has been a self-delusion.   It is a continuing Methodism into which we E.U.B.'s have merged our identity.   There should be no grief on that account, for the Master has said that to lose ones' life is to find it.[37]

This discussion of the 1968 union/merger of E.U.B.'s and Methodists is by no means conclusive; an in-depth study on this subject would result in a volume written by an expert in the field. This is but a brief over-view of the issues involved, but hopefully it conveys that this was an issue that engaged not just the mind but the very heart and soul - indeed the very existence - of the Evangelical United Brethren Church.

There were other major issues that had faced the Evangelical/E.U.B. Church in its more than a century and a half of existence.   One was the split in the 1890s, resulting in the Evangelical Association and the United Evangelical Church who then reunited in 1922. Another was the German/English language issue, and a third was the 1946 union of the Evangelical Church and the United Brethren in Christ, resulting in the Evangelical United Brethren Church.   All three of these major issues caused some dissension, anger and trauma for the church at the national level, in specific conferences, and at the congregational level.   A time of healing and reconciliation was then necessary, and it often took years to bring this about.

The German/English language issue was perhaps the one which next to the union/merger issue with the Methodists had the most impact and importance for the future of the church. Certainly this was true in Minnesota, where the 1890s split and reunion in 1922, and the 1946 union were not as traumatic as in many other areas.

The German/English language issue and the 1968 union/merger with the Methodist Church were similar in that proponents of German or those opposed to union/merger in 1968 believed that their church would truly no longer really exist if their cause went down to defeat. And this was true to a certain extent, for surely the Evangelische Gemeinschaft *did* lose part of its heritage when it made the change to English and the future. It was no less true for the union/merger of 1968, for surely the E.U.B. Church *did* cease to exist as such when the United Methodist Church became a reality. How this new church – and more specifically the prairie churches in this study – developed in new ways and maintained ties to its past, will be the subject of the next chapter.

Notes

[1] "Conference Rushes to a Close," *The Telescope Messenger,* Vol. 124, No. 45 (Nov. 8, 1958), p. 14.

[2] W. Cecil Findley, "Let's Get Together," *The Telescope Messenger*, Vol. 124, No. 15 (April 12, 1958), p. 6-8.

3 F. Gerald Ensley, "The Methodists Speak to Evangelical United Brethren," *The Telescope Messenger*, Vol. 124, No. 46 (Nov. 15, 1958), p. 7-8.

4 Kenneth W. Krueger, "Is There a Future for the Evangelical United Brethren Church?" *The Telescope Messenger*, Vol. 126, No. 5 (March 5, 1960), p. 8,12.

5 Joe Willard Krecker, "Our Most Recent Invitation to Church Union," *The Telescope Messenger*, Vol. 128, No. 11 (May 26, 1962), p. 27.

6 G. Weir Hartman and John K. Bergland, "Shall General Conference Authorize a Basis of Union with the Methodists?" *The Telescope Messenger*, Vol. 128, No. 19 (Sept. 15, 1962) pp. 14-17.

7 Hartman, *Ibid.,* p. 16.

8 Bergland, *Ibid.,* pp. 15, 17.

9 Paul A. Washburn, "Three Words of Caution on the Subject of Possible Union with the Methodists," *The Telescope Messenger*, Vol. 129, No. 3 (Feb. 2, 1963), p. 16.

10 "Joint Commission Meeting at Cleveland Advances Prospect of Union with Methodists," *The Telescope Messenger*, Vol. 129, No. 9 (April 27, 1963), p. 13.

11 Joe Willard Krecker, "Let's Join the Methodists in Observance of Aldersgate Year," *The Telescope Messenger*, Vol. 129, No. 7 (March 30, 1963, p. 27.

12 Joe Willard Krecker, "Looking Toward Union," *Church and Home*, Feb. 15, 1964, p. 22.

13 William E. Sherriff, "Letters," *Church and Home*, May 15, 1964, p. 32.

14 Bishop H. R. Heininger, *Minnesota Conference Official Record–1964* (Harrisburg, 1964), p. 57.

15 Floyd E. Bosshardt, 1962 Report of the Conference Director of Christian Education-Misssions, *Minnesota Conference Official Record–1962* (Harrisburg, 1962), p. 81.

16 A. B. Utzman and E. R. Praetorius, Report of the Conference Superintendents, *Minnesota Conference Official Record–1962* (Harrisburg, 1962), p. 68.

17 *Ibid.*, p. 69.

18 *Ibid.*, (1961), p. 66.

19 *Ibid.*, p. 69.

20 *Ibid.*, (1965), p. 74.

21 *Ibid.*

22 *Ibid.*

23 *Ibid.*, (1961), p. 66.

24 "Basis of Union, New Grove EUB Church and Hendricks Methodist Church, Hendricks, Minnesota," pp. 1-2, Hendricks Zion (New Grove) records.

25 Willard M. Mecklenburg, "Where We Stand on Union," *Together*, April 1963, p. 34.

26 Harvey M. Chinn, "Fourteen to One: The Odds of Merger," *Church and Home*, Sept. 1, 1966, p. 17.

27 C. R. Findley, "Fifteen Plus One: Opportunity for Renewal," *Church and Home*, Sept. 1, 1966, p. 18.

28 Etta A. Petzoldt, "Letters," *Church and Home*, Nov. 15, 1965, pp. 32-33.

29 Lowell Reader, "Letters," *Church and Home*, Feb. 15, 1967, p. 33.

30 E. Russell Praetorius, "Union Editorial Challenged...," *Minnesota Conference News Review*, Vol. 18, No. 2 (November 1966), p. 2.

31 Ray Boehlke, Report of the Special Committee on Church Union and Renewal to the Minnesota Evangelical United Brethren Conference Council on Administration - July 7, 1965, *Minnesota Conference Official Record–1966* (Harrisburg, 1966), pp. 107-109.

32 "General Conference Approves Church Union," *Church and Home*, Dec. 15, 1966, p. 22.

33 "Methodist - EUB Union Timetable," *Church and Home,* Feb 1, 1967, p. 31.

34 Resolution on the Union of the Methodist Church and the Evangelical United Brethren Church, *Minnesota Conference Official Record–1967* (Harrisburg, 1967), p. 64.

35 Paige Carlin, "A New Church is Born," *Together*, Vol. 12, (May 1968), p. 20.

36 Curtis A. Chambers, "A New Church," *Church and Home,* June 1968, p. 3.

37 Joe Willard Krecker, "Joy...Unity...Service...Today," *Church and Home*, June 1968, p. 25.

Chapter Eight

United Methodism on the Minnesota Prairie: 1969 – 1998

Structural Union Becomes Reality

While the Uniting Conference took place in Dallas in April 1968, the real form and substance required to give meaning to merger/union would need to develop over time. This would have to take place on a national level, in the many conferences throughout the country, and within the individual churches and congregations themselves.

It is not within the scope of this study to discuss the many changes required on a national level. It must be remembered, however, that included in these changes were such things as the continued existence or realignment of denominational colleges and seminaries, and the development of new denominational publications, literature, and hymnals. These changes, among many others, would be felt very directly at both the state and local levels in the years to come.

In Minnesota, the former E.U.B. Conference of the new United Methodist Church met in May 1968, and the new church was much on the minds of those present. As the Report of the District Superintendents put it:

> This past year we have experienced the passing of the old and we hopefully accept the new. The birth of the United Methodist Church on April 23rd brought a great change into the life of our Church and into the life of each one of us who were former members of the Evangelical United Brethren Church. We would be hypocritical if we would say that it has been easy and smooth. Mixed feelings lie upon our hearts as we sense in some the restlessness, the attitudes, and reluctant heart as we experience this union. We confess that there are many things about the union and the new structure that disturb us also. We know that continued changes will affect every church and member...[1]

The Superintendents then stressed the need for a fellowship of earnest and sincere prayer within the Conference, to help "...break down walls of suspicion, unfair criticism, prejudices, or jealousies that may exist."[2]

Conference leadership expressed a clear understanding of the multi-faceted tasks of union, and also a sincere desire to do the work necessary for this major endeavor. A Plan and Basis of

Union for the E.U.B. and Methodist conferences of the United Methodist Church in Minnesota was developed and presented to the two conferences for approval. This Plan and Basis for Union in Minnesota laid out the mechanics and timetable for the practical aspects of union. It included provisions such as that initially there would be twice the actual ratio of E.U.B.'s to Methodists on all boards, commissions and committees. Thus, since the ratio in Minnesota was eight Methodists to one E.U.B., this meant that initially E.U.B. representation would be one in four.[3] This Plan and Basis for Union was then voted on by the two conferences in Spring 1969; the Methodists voted unanimously to accept the Plan, while the E.U.B. vote was 118 "yes" and 9 "no."[4] Work on structural union between the two conferences in Minnesota proceeded, and the two conferences officially became one in 1970. Working out the specifics of this union would of course take time; this was even more true at the regional and local levels.

There were many variables to be considered in each particular area, be it urban, suburban, small town or rural. These variables included such things as proximity of former E.U.B. and Methodist churches, the relative size, strength and vitality of these churches, the receptivity of local congregations to the United Methodist union itself and to changes both large and small. More general issues, such as rural to urban/suburban movement and declining rural population, a general decline in church membership and hence of resources available to churches, and a continuing shortage of ministers also played major roles in the unfolding of the new United Methodist Church in Minnesota.

United Methodism took widely varying forms in the three

different geographical areas studied, depending on their past history and the combination of the variables discussed above. Each area and each congregation within that area had its own unique history and place within the Minnesota Conference, be it Evangelical, E.U.B. or now United Methodist. How the former E.U.B. churches in these three areas now became a part of United Methodism will be the focus of the remainder of this chapter.

Former E.U.B./United Methodist Churches in South Central Minnesota

There were six former E.U.B. churches in Faribault County in 1968. These were Wells Evangelical (which had been called Wells E.U.B. after Dunbar Zion joined them in 1954 and before that had been Wells Salem), Rice Lake Emmanuel (with which Brush Creek Tabor united in 1957), Blue Earth Immanuel, Blue Earth Salem, and the two former U.B. churches, Kiester Grace (served jointly with Rice Lake since 1967) and Pleasant Prairie. The Kiester and Pleasant Prairie churches are not discussed below since neither were original Evangelical churches in Faribault County.

The two United Methodist churches in Wells were both good-sized churches; Wells Evangelical had 343 members, while the former Methodist church, Central, had 446 members. These two churches had had friendly and close relationships for many years. The Evangelical (formerly Salem) congregation had the newer building, having built a new and larger church in 1957. Central's building was a lovely old historic edifice built in 1897 and their congregation chose to remain separate when invited to unite with Wells Evangelical. The two churches continued to cooperate in many ways, and in 1970 they appointed committees to further joint activities and to look at the feasibility of an eventual union.[5] Then in April 1973, Central's building burned, suffering extensive interior damage.[6] It was then decided after much discussion and many meetings, that Central would unite with Evangelical, a decision that no doubt was very difficult for some of Central's members. The two churches then united in September 1973, forming the Wells United Methodist Church.

The Wells United Methodist Church was then served by one senior minister and an associate minister until 1987. At that time, due to financial concerns (the farm crisis of the 1980s was having a negative effect in the area) it was decided to go with one minister and sell the former Methodist parsonage. An addition to the church was built in 1989, and Wells United Methodist continues to serve the area that its predecessors had served since Dunbar Zion Evangelical Church was founded in 1865.

The Rice Lake Emmanuel Church was still a strong rural church in the late 1960s; its membership was 149 in 1968. And while the decline in rural population had certainly had an effect (membership had been 166 in 1961), Rice Lake still had some younger families in its membership and was looking to the future and not to the past. The Rice Lake and Kiester churches continued to be served by one minister.

The major issue for the Rice Lake church came to the fore in the 1980s. A former E.U.B. minister had been appointed to Rice Lake/Kiester in 1975. By the early 1980s he had formed a charismatic Bible study group within the congregation. As time went on, this group became more and more secretive, and separate from the rest of the congregation. It seemed apparent to some of those who were not in the charismatic group that this group led by the pastor and his wife intended to establish a new and non-United Methodist center of some kind. Contacts were made with Conference leadership in 1983 to apprise them of the divisive nature of the charismatic group, and while the leadership did finally respond and take action, it was too late to prevent a major split. In 1984 the charismatic group took almost half of the church's membership with them and formed their own separate non-United Methodist congregation.

This major division in the Rice Lake church had, as indicated, been building for some time. Families were pitted against one another, neighbors were on opposite sides of the issue, and the hurt and bitterness engendered would last for years. With the split, membership had gone from 117 to 68 in 1984, and then continued a gradual decline. In any case, Rice Lake Emmanuel (with 46 members) and Kiester Grace (with 92 members) became a "blended" congregation in 1996 whereby their organizations and memberships were merged but both churches remained open.

Blue Earth Immanuel, the oldest Evangelical congregation in Faribault County, was in some ways similar to Rice Lake in that it too was located near a town with a larger sister church, (Blue Earth Salem) but was not served by the same minister. Having been one of the largest Evangelical churches in Minnesota in very early years (prior to 1900) it had held its own, but certainly reflected the changing rural scene. This church still had 150 members in 1968, but with the continuing decline in rural population (Faribault County was hit hard by the farm crisis in the 1980s) membership had declined to 77 in 1998. The congregation has been jointly served with the Delavan (formerly Methodist) congregation since 1978.

The problems and issues faced by Blue Earth Immanuel can be seen in many other of the rural or smaller congregations; i.e., it is often difficult to attract new members and/or to keep young families in the congregation when larger United Methodist churches are nearby which have more resources and programs to offer. It does not necessarily follow, however, that these small churches have outlived their usefulness. Blue Earth Immanuel now serves primarily an older congregation, but it remains a living witness.

Blue Earth Salem, located in the town of Blue Earth, was the largest of the Evangelical/E.U.B. churches in Faribault County and one of the largest in the Minnesota Conference. It was a prosperous congregation, and had built a beautiful new church in 1942. The First Methodist Church in Blue Earth was similar in size to Blue Earth Salem; when the United Methodist Church was formed in 1968, First Methodist had 442 members and Salem E.U.B. had 393 members.

Salem and First churches have maintained separate identities until recently, with each church served by a full-time minister. Economic factors and decline in population contributed to some concerns regarding keeping up two totally separate congregations, and in 1996, one minister was appointed to serve both Salem and First churches in a "blend" arrangement similar to that for Rice Lake/Kiester where both churches will remain open, but memberships and organizations merged.

Former E.U.B./United Methodists
in Southwest Minnesota

The adaptation to United Methodism in southwest Minnesota followed a somewhat different course than in Faribault County, primarily because most of the E.U.B. churches in southwest Minnesota were considerably smaller than their Methodist counterparts. It must also be remembered that this area as a whole continued to lose population at a greater rate than did Faribault County.

The Fairmont Salem Church had never been a large one, and had 96 members in 1968. Fairmont's Methodist church was much larger, with 1,258 members in 1968. As merger/union talks between the E.U.B.'s and Methodists had accelerated in the mid-1960s, so too did similar discussions emerge between the two denominations' churches in Fairmont. In March 1968 both the E.U.B.'s and Methodists voted favorably for a united congregation, and in June 1968 the E.U.B.'s joined the Methodists in the United Methodist Church of Fairmont.

Welcome Emmanuel had always been served with Fairmont Salem, but the Welcome congregation was not drawn toward union with the Methodists. This congregation had historically been theologically conservative, and when the national union became reality they requested that their minister be a former E.U.B. Conference responded by appointing a former E.U.B. minister to serve as Associate Pastor of Education in the Fairmont church; this former E.U.B. would serve the Welcome church. This changed the next year, when Welcome Emmanuel was jointly served with the former Methodist Welcome and Sherburn churches.

176

Welcome Emmanuel's membership was 43 in 1968, and membership stayed about the same thereafter. Some families left Emmanuel when it became a United Methodist church, feeling that in good conscience they could not become United Methodists. Welcome Emmanuel continued to struggle and in all sincerity to remain true to what its remaining members felt was important to their faith. Notes from Emmanuel's Administrative Board Meeting of July 20, 1983 stated: "We discussed the need for spiritual renewal here in Emmanuel, both in the congregation in general, and in the Sunday School. The meeting closed with a session of heartfelt prayer, and earnest tears were shed..."[7]

It was just two years later that Welcome Emmanuel Church closed. The last service was held on June 30, 1985, with most remaining members transferring to non-United Methodist churches. The building was sold in 1986 to Heritage Acres, an historic pioneer village reconstruction in nearby Fairmont, and has been used as a non-denominational chapel since 1989. One does not have to agree with the theological or religious views of most of Emmanuel's members to share in the sadness that accompanied the closing of this rural church.

The former E.U.B. church in Worthington was Emmanuel; its membership in 1968 was 194. The First Methodist Church in Worthington was much larger with 932 members in 1968, but the two churches remained separate after the 1968 union. The nearby Bigelow United Methodist Church was then served with Worthington Emmanuel from 1970 to 1984. In 1985 the Bigelow church closed, and one senior minister and an associate minister were assigned to Worthington First and Worthington Emmanuel.

As has been true for so many other small churches, Worthington Emmanuel finds it difficult to attract new members and families with small children, when the much larger former Methodist church has more resources and programs to offer. Emmanuel's membership, however, continues to enjoy the friendship and fellowship that a smaller church can offer, and thus chooses to continue as a separate congregation.

As was noted in the previous chapter, the Luverne Ebenezer (Pleasant View) Church had moved (albeit reluctantly) from its rural birthplace into a new building in the town of Luverne in 1955. This venture did not thrive, and this church closed only ten years later in 1965; membership had gone from 51 in 1955 to 30 in 1965. Members then transferred to the Steen Salem Church, or to Methodist or other denominations. The Steen Salem Church which had been served by the same minister as the Luverne church continued on, although without a regular minister and under the care of the District Superintendent. After the E.U.B./Methodist union in 1968, the Steen church closed and merged with the Luverne First United Methodist Church in their new building in November, 1969.

In the Pipestone area there were still two E.U.B. churches at the time of the 1968 union. These were Pipestone Zion (in town) and rural Pipestone Salem; they had historically been served by one minister and this still was the case in 1968. There were three Methodist churches in the area also; a large congregation (Peace) in Pipestone, and two smaller churches (Jasper and Trosky) nearby. How best to meet the needs of these five United Methodist churches was discussed in a series of meetings in 1969. The decisions made called for Peace and Trosky to be served by one minister, and for Zion, Salem and Jasper to be a three-point charge with one minister.

The Zion congregation had built a new church in Pipestone in 1960. Some decline in membership began after the 1968 union, in part because Zion could not offer the variety of programs available in the larger church. As was the case in several other towns, this former E.U.B. church was much smaller (there were 154 members in 1968) than its former Methodist counterpart which had 807 members in 1968. Then also, starting in the mid-1970s, a succession of ministers was assigned to Zion, Salem and Jasper. This was not helpful to Zion at a time when it needed stability and leadership. Zion's members tried very hard to persevere, but were not able to do so. Zion held its last service on July 31, 1993; a majority of its members transferred to Peace United Methodist, while some went to Salem, or to the Presbyterian church.

The rural Pipestone Salem Church continues in existence, and is again part of a three-point charge, being served with Jasper, and with the United Church of Garretson, South Dakota. As has been the case with so many of the small rural churches, its membership has continued to decline along with the rural population in the area. This church's members are still primarily of German descent, with many of its members belonging to inter-related family groups.

Another former E.U.B. church located close to the South Dakota border was Hendricks Zion (New Grove). This was a rural church, and it was not located near any other E.U.B. churches.

179

Hence it had sometimes been difficult for Conference to assign a full-time minister there, and this church was sometimes served by a ministerial student.

As was indicated in the last chapter, there was movement toward cooperation and possible later union with the Hendricks Methodist Church even before the national union between E.U.B.'s and Methodists. A tentative Basis of Union was drawn up in 1966, whereby the two churches would become Grace United Church of Hendricks, which would be part of the Minnesota E.U.B. Conference.[8] The Hendricks New Grove vote in March 1968 for union with the Methodist Church in town was 34 "yes" and 27 "no,"[9] clearly indicating a congregation divided on the issue. The union did take place and Grace United was officially an E.U.B. Church until 1970 when the Methodist and E.U.B. conferences became United Methodists in Minnesota. The Hendricks Grace minister also serves the United Methodist Church in nearby Ivanhoe. Grace Church now occupies the former First Lutheran Church building in Hendricks; the old New Grove Church was dismantled, and in the words of a long time New Grove member:

> Old neighbors and former members occasionally drive past the grove in the northwest corner of Shoakatan township, the only visible reminder of New Grove Evangelical Church and its site; and despite the years since its demise, there is always a pang of nostalgia. In itself, it was a landmark. It still lives in the hearts of those who were confirmed and married there, whose children have been baptized there, and whose parents' funerals were conducted

there. The most tangible remnant is the cemetery about a mile from the church site where crumbling headstones recall the names of pioneer German families in the New Grove Community.[10]

It should be noted here that Zion (New Grove) Evangelical/E.U.B., now Grace United Methodist, members do not just look back; they also look ahead to the future, as shown in their support of the decision in the mid-1990s to rebuild the church steeple. Discussion on this issue centered on whether a new steeple made sense in a day of declining membership, but hope for the continued life of their church prevailed.

The last church in southwest Minnesota to be discussed is Marshall Albright (formerly Salem), the largest of the former E.U.B. churches in this area. This church had 191 members in 1968 while Wesley Methodist had 607. Marshall Salem E.U.B. had been joined by the Clifton Bethel members when the rural Clifton church closed in 1947, and a new church was built in Marshall in 1954. This congregation was then known as the Marshall E.U.B. Church, and then chose the name Marshall Albright after the E.U.B. union with the Methodist church in 1968. After the 1968 national union, the small Lynd (formerly Methodist) congregation was served with Marshall Albright. The Lynd congregation was dissolved in 1994, with most members transferring their membership to Albright. The two United Methodist churches in Marshall reflect their distinct heritages in their names – Albright and Wesley – and provide a joint United Methodist witness in Marshall.

Former E.U.B./United Methodist Churches
in Western Minnesota

Of the six Evangelical churches originally in this area, three were gone before the 1968 union. These three were: rural Salem (in Yellowbank Township) which had closed in 1931 and merged with Bellingham Zion; Fairfield Zion which had closed in 1940, with most of its remaining members going to the Appleton Methodist Church; and Yellowbank Emmanuel which had just closed in 1962 and joined with the Odessa congregation to form Odessa Hope, using the Yellowbank building which had been moved into Odessa. Thus, Bellingham Zion, Madison Ebenezer, and Odessa Hope were still open in 1968. It should be noted that the small Correll church was still open also. Correll, as noted previously, was not included in this study since it wasn't an official appointment of the Evangelical Church in 1922.

By the late 1960s further changes for the remaining churches in this area were in the making. This was an area where population had been declining for some time with farms getting larger and many young people having to move away in order to make a living. It could be expected that all of the churches, not just the E.U.B.'s, in this area would also be experiencing difficulties.

As was mentioned in the last chapter, Reverend Ted Colescott of Clinton Methodist and Graceville United Church of Christ and Reverend Dwight Haberman of Ortonville Methodist invited seventeen E.U.B., Methodist, United Church of Christ and Presbyterian ministers and their congregations to a meeting in February 1967. All seventeen churches were represented at this meeting. Consultations continued and eight of the original seventeen churches joined to form the Minnesota River Headwaters Parish in April 1969. Three more churches joined by 1972, and four of the total of eleven were former E.U.B., now United Methodist churches in the area. These were the Bellingham, Correll, Odessa and Madison churches.[11]

Headwaters Parish programs included shared ministries, a parish office and secretary, camps and vacation church schools, musical programs, and parish-wide confirmation classes. Over the next fifteen years (1972-1987) Headwaters Parish continued to function, although some churches left and others closed. It was finally decided to disband Headwaters Parish; this took place in May 1987.

Returning to the former E.U.B., now United Methodist churches in the area, Bellingham Zion, Madison Ebenezer and Odessa Hope churches were a three-point charge between 1971 and 1982. Membership in all the churches was declining, with the largest decline in Odessa Hope's membership in these years. In addition to the population decline due to larger farms, there was also displacement due to farm land reclaimed for the Big Stone National Wildlife Refuge.

The Odessa Hope Church was closed in May 1982 and its members transferred to Bellingham Zion, Big Stone City (South Dakota) Tabor (both formerly E.U.B.) or to Ortonville United Methodist. For those who had been members of Yellowbank Emmanuel at its closing in 1962 and then of Odessa Hope until its closing in 1982, one should hardly wonder if they experienced a sense of displacement since they were now forced to join yet a third church. It is worthwhile to remember that though there are usually rational reasons for church closings, those who lose their church and must begin again at another may see the issue in a different light.

Bellingham Zion and Madison Ebenezer were then served by one minister between 1982 and 1992. Since 1992 they have been served with Appleton (formerly Methodist) United Methodist in a three-point charge. Being part of a three-point charge is not easy for either the minister or the congregations; this is as true in 1998 as it was in 1868. Each church prefers particular times for Sunday services and other activities, and these preferences cannot always be met. Compromises must be made by all concerned, and cooperation becomes a necessity, not a goal. Both the Bellingham and Madison churches have primarily aging and declining memberships, so there is concern for the future while they still strive to meet needs and provide a witness for the current time.

Summary

This survey of the former E.U.B. churches in south central, southwestern and western Minnesota is not intended to give an up-to-the minute account of how each church is doing as the twentieth century draws to a close. Rather, it is an attempt to point out how different churches in each of the three areas adapted to being United Methodist churches and to other factors which have affected them in the last thirty years.

As we have seen in south central Minnesota, one town church (Wells) is now the home for the joined congregations that were previously Wells Salem/Evangelical and Wells Central Methodist. In Blue Earth, both the former Methodist and E.U.B.

Church Membership: South Central Minnesota

Church	1968	1970	1975	1980	1985	1990	1995	1998
Blue Earth Imm.	150	154	132	127	115	87	82	77
Blue Earth Sal.	393	382	401	422	382	303	246	209
Rice Lake	149	134	129	114	68 [a]	75	46	137 [b]
Wells	343	320	704 [c]	659	600	542	470	465
Totals	1035	990	1366	1322	1165	1007	844	888

Church Membership: Southwest Minnesota

Church	1968	1970	1975	1980	1985	1990	1995	1998
Fairmont	96	(d)						
Welcome	43	40	43	46	44	(e)		
Worthington	194	180	159	129	116	88	65	67
Steen	54	(f)						
Pipestone Salem	65	61	55	54	42	34	30	28
Pipestone Zion	154	144	152	167	151	111	(g)	
Hendricks	128	192 [h]	171	191	170	154	140	121
Marshall	191	204	231	257	249	246	228	226
Totals	925	821	811	844	772	633	463	442

Church Membership: Western Minnesota

Church	1968	1970	1975	1980	1985	1990	1995	1998
Madison	104	111	80	92	73	67	62	53
Bellingham	138	126	78	78	67	63	54	51
Odessa Hope	74	66	51	37	(i)			
Totals	316	303	209	207	140	130	116	104

| Grand Totals | 2276 | 2114 | 2386 | 2373 | 2077 | 1770 | 1423 | 1434 |

[a]Rice Lake – congregational split in 1984 (See pp. 173-174) resulted in loss of membership. [b]Rice Lake – in "blended" congregation with Kiester Grace since 1996. [c]Wells– Central U.M. united with Salem Evangelical U.M. in 1973 to form Wells U.M.. [d]Fairmont – closed and joined Fairmont U.M. in 1968. [e]Welcome – closed in 1985; most members transferred to other denominations. [f]Steen – closed and joined Luverne First U.M. in 1969. [g]Pipestone Zion – closed in 1993; most members transferred to Pipestone Peace U.M.. [h]Hendricks Zion and Hendricks Methodist united in 1970 to form Hendricks Grace U.M. [i]Odessa – closed in 1982; most members transferred to Bellingham, Big Stone City, S.D., or Ortonville U.M..

churches continue to function although they are now served by one minister. The two rural churches (Rice Lake Emmanuel and Blue Earth Immanuel) both experienced large membership declines, due to farm population decline, and for Rice Lake, a split within the congregation as well.

The churches in southwest Minnesota show a wide variety of changes and adaptations. Welcome Emmanuel struggled both with declining population/membership issues and with United Methodism; this church closed in 1985. The Pipestone Salem Church continues and is served with two other small churches, one United Methodist and one United Church of Christ. The Hendricks church was already yoked with the town Methodist church in 1968; these two churches became Grace United Methodist (albeit with some misgivings on the part of some) by 1970. The Luverne E.U.B. church had closed in 1965, and Steen Salem merged with the large First United Methodist Church in Luverne in 1969.

The other four former E.U.B. churches in southwest Minnesota were all located in towns of some size, but none of them had over 200 members at the time of the 1968 union. The Fairmont Salem Church actually merged with the much larger Fairmont Methodist Church before the United Methodist Church in Minnesota became a reality. Worthington Emmanuel remains as a separate congregation from the much larger First United Methodist Church; they are currently served by one minister and a former E.U.B. associate minister. Pipestone Zion was forced to close in 1993; most of its members joined Peace United Methodist Church in Pipestone. And Marshall Albright (formerly

Salem E.U.B.) is served by its own minister while Marshall Wesley (formerly Methodist) also has its own minister.

In western Minnesota, Odessa Hope (made up of the former Odessa Salem and Yellowbank Emmanuel congregations) was forced to close in 1982. With Bellingham Zion and Madison Ebenezer, these churches participated in the innovative Headwaters Parish in that area between 1969 and 1987 when the parish disbanded. Both Bellingham Zion and Madison Ebenezer remain open; there were no United Methodist congregations in either town before the 1968 union. They are now served as part of a three-point charge with the Appleton United Methodist Church.

It is clear that there were many different ways for churches in these three areas to adapt to United Methodism. Each church had members who had supported the 1968 union with Methodism and members who ranged from mildly to adamantly opposed to that union. It can be assumed that all of these churches, in each of the three different areas, had to struggle with feelings of loss of identity and of their Evangelical/E.U.B. heritages as they became part of a much larger group in United Methodism. What these struggles meant, whether and how they have been resolved, and what was gained and what was lost as E.U.B.'s became United Methodists on the prairies of Minnesota will be the subject of the next and last chapter.

Notes

1 E. Russell Praetorius and Gerald V. Walder, Report of the District Superintendents, *Minnesota Conference Official Record–1968* (Harrisburg, 1968), pp. 68-69.

2 *Ibid.*, p. 69.

3 Boards, Commissions, Committees; Plan and Basis for Union, *Minnesota Conference Official Record–1969* (Rochester, 1969) p. 388-389.

4 Official Proceedings, *Ibid.*, p. 190.

5 Rosamond Miller, "The E.U.B. Church," *The United Methodist Church of Wells 125th Anniversary, 1865-1990*, p. 18, Wells records.

6 Jessie Parriott, "Central United Methodist Church," *Ibid.*, p. 11, Wells records.

7 Minnesota United Methodist Conference Records, Administrative Board Minutes, Welcome Emmanuel UMC, 1870-1985; Box 8, Folder 4.

8 "Basis of Union, New Grove Evangelical United Brethren Church and Hendricks Methodist Church, Hendricks, Minnesota," p. 1, Hendricks Zion (New Grove) records.

9 Committee on Boundaries, *Minnesota Conference Official Record–1968* (Harrisburg, 1968) p. 110.

10 "New Grove E.U.B. Church History," p. 1, Hendricks Zion (New Grove) records.

11 "Headwaters Parish," *Zion United Methodist Church, 1889-1989*, p. 44, Bellingham Zion records.

Chapter Nine

Still Marching Through
Immanuel's Ground

Introduction

This study of the Evangelical Church on the Minnesota prairie has attempted to show what happens to an immigrant church over time. More specifically, it has addressed the question of what happened to the Evangelische Gemeinschaft in Minnesota as it became the Evangelical Association/Church, then the Evangelical United Brethren Church, and finally merged with the Methodists to become part of the United Methodist Church.

This chapter will now look at and reflect upon the different aspects of this evolvement from the Evangelische Gemeinschaft to United Methodist Church, as it took place more generally and on the Minnesota prairie.

Who Were the Evangelicals
and What was Important to Them

Before looking at the Evangelicals in Minnesota, it behooves us to look back at who these Evangelicals were in the first place, and at what was important to them. As discussed in Chapter One, the early Evangelicals were part of a religious movement which took place in the newly-formed United States in the late eighteenth and early nineteenth centuries. Other similar groups were the Methodists, and the United Brethren in Christ. The founder of the Evangelical Association, or Evangelische Gemeinschaft as it was then called, was Jacob Albright. His mission, and that of the Evangelicals who followed him, was to preach the Christian gospel with special emphasis on reaching German immigrants who were not being ministered to in their own language.

As the Evangelische Gemeinschaft took form and substance, it became clear that certain beliefs and behaviors were of great importance to Evangelicals. As Kenneth Krueger indicates, these included a personal experience of God in conversion and a personal faith. The major hallmarks of this faith were a sense of reverence for God and all creation, and for the Scriptures. There was an emphasis on personal piety which included a strong prayer and devotional life, holy living and high ethical behavior. There was also some sense of being "set apart" and of anti-worldliness or of being "in the world but not of it."[1]

The German "Evangelische Gemeinschaft" was translated into the "Evangelical Association" in English, but might more accurately have been translated into "Evangelical Community" or "Fellowship." Another German word or concept, "Gemutlichkeit," meaning a "kind disposition" or "friendliness" was important to Evangelicals as well. And finally, the "Gesangbuch" or hymnbook, was of great importance to Evangelicals, as they expressed their faith in song both reverently and joyfully. These emphases, described above, resulted in what at its best was, in Krueger's words, "a warm and intimate spiritual fellowship."[2]

Certainly all Evangelicals and/or churches did not live up to what their faith and beliefs asked of them. Differing interpretations of what the church and/or Scriptures meant sometimes resulted in rancor and division; the 1890s split into the Evangelical Association and the United Evangelicals was a stark example of this. Moral issues were important to Evangelicals, and such behaviors as drinking alcohol, smoking, gambling, social dancing or divorce were seen as harmful to oneself and others. And sometimes judgmental self-righteousness took precedence over hating the sin and not the sinner, and resulted in people being permanently lost to the church.

The Evangelical Church continued to change and grow, and as the twentieth century evolved increasing emphasis was placed on the social gospel along with individual salvation. As Behney and Eller state:

> By the end of the last century a new, virile emphasis was heard among Evangelicals for which there was no denominational precedent. Salvation, it held, was available for men individually and corporately. The gospel was pertinent to life and all of life - a perspective which emerged as more people became aware of gross inequities and injustices... In 1913 the episcopal message declared the success of

Christianity was to be measured not by the numbers on the church rolls, but by its leavening influence in transforming society... For a time the tensions between the individual and the social gospel persisted, but by 1920 this was subsiding with the recognition that the two were neither adversaries nor alternatives, but two aspects of one gospel.[3]

This is not to say that there was one accepted Evangelical understanding of the importance of personal salvation or of social action for the church. There were individual church congregations and members who felt that personal salvation was of far greater importance than was social action; this view was exemplified in the E.U.B. Conferences on the West Coast and Montana who voted not to join the United Methodist Church in 1968. There were individuals and churches with similar views in Minnesota, but Conference leadership and action gave credence to both as part of the Christian gospel.

Reflections on the Evangelical/E.U.B. Church on the Minnesota Prairie

In looking at the Evangelical and then E.U.B. Church on the Minnesota prairie from its pioneer beginnings in the 1850s through its becoming part of the United Methodist Church one can see times of growth and unity of purpose, and others where conflicts had to be resolved. The one constant was change, as the Evangelische Gemeinshaft moved through time and went from being an immigrant church to merger with a mainstream denomination. And while there was always continuity within change and some overlap, there seem to be four main time periods which encompass these changes. These will be discussed below, as we reflect on the meaning of the Evangelical/E.U.B. Church on the Minnesota prairie.

The Evangelische Gemeinschaft: 1856 - 1890

Pioneer times for the Evangelical Church, or Evangelische Gemeinschaft as it was then known, are covered in Chapters Two and Three. The mid-and-late nineteenth century was a time of great growth for the Evangelische Gemeinschaft, since large numbers of new German immigrants arrived in the United States during that time period. These immigrants came for a variety of reasons: some to escape political oppression or long terms of mandatory military service; others came for economic reasons and to acquire land.

Acquiring farmland was the major reason most German immigrants came to the frontier Midwest in the latter decades of the nineteenth century. They bought land, which was relatively cheap, or after 1862 often acquired it by meeting the requirements of the Homestead Act. As was discussed in Chapter Two, pioneer life was often fraught with hardships and difficulties. But there were good times in pioneer life too, as families and neighbors worked together in the development of their farms and communities.

Churches played a major role in this process, and the Evangelische Gemeinschaft was quick to respond to the call for their ministry to German-speaking immigrants in the Midwest. An Evangelical minister (Andrew Tarnutzer) first came to Minnesota Territory in 1856, and others soon followed. Each decade then saw Evangelical growth, as Minnesota Evangelicals numbered 5,901 by 1890.

During these years, circuit-riding Evangelical ministers established "classes" of Evangelical members on the Minnesota prairies. Small rural churches were built by these Evangelicals as soon as possible, usually on land donated by one of the members. And while some Evangelical classes or appointments failed to thrive, many grew and prospered by the later decades of the nineteenth century. Evangelical churches were being established in towns and villages as well as in the country, in primarily the southern one-third of Minnesota. The Evangelical churches of south central, southwestern and western Minnesota were established in these years. In fact in 1883, a new Dakota Conference was established as Evangelicals moved still further west.

The written accounts of Evangelicals in Minnesota in these early years both in Conference Journals and local records, convey optimism and a clear sense of mission. Evangelical ministers were intent on spreading the gospel to German immigrants. There were setbacks such as the loss of Evangelicals in the Dakota Conflict of 1862, and less traumatic setbacks where new Evangelical classes and appointments did not thrive. But the overall impression is of a church on the move in Minnesota, with virtually unlimited faith in its future.

The Evangelical Association: 1891 -1921

As is true of most human endeavors, religious or otherwise, forward progress is often thwarted by human frailties as well as by events beyond human control. As discussed in Chapter Four, this was certainly the case for the Evangelical Association on a national level, as major power struggles between two bishops (Escher and Dubs) resulted in rancorous division in the mid-1890s. Bishop Dubs' group formed the new United Evangelical Church, while the majority (about three-fifths) stayed on with Bishop Escher in the Evangelical Association. This was not a time when principles of Christian forbearance were evident within the church itself. Fortunately both groups were able to reconsider and to realize that they were one in spirit, and the two churches reunited in 1922 in Detroit, Michigan.

The Evangelical division of the 1890s did not impact Minnesota as much as in more eastern states, since most Minnesota Evangelicals remained in the Evangelical Association. There were a few United Evangelical churches started in western Minnesota, however, one of which was the church in Odessa which then became an Evangelical church in the 1922 reunification.

An issue of major impact for the Evangelical Association in Minnesota as the twentieth century approached was that German immigration had slowed to a trickle. With few Germans now moving into Minnesota, the establishment and rapid growth of new Evangelical churches slowed down considerably. Thus, this was a time of steady but not spectacular growth and solidification. Some churches outgrew their first buildings, dismantled them and shipped them off to a smaller congregation, and then built a new church. Others added onto existing structures, modernizing as they did so.

The issue of most importance to Minnesota Evangelicals during these decades (1891-1921) was that of the use of German versus English in the churches. As discussed in Chapter Four, this issue was fought out congregation by congregation, and most traumatically within congregations. Many older members continued to proclaim "Wir sind Deutsch, und Deutsch werden wir bleiben" ("We are German and we will remain German.") Younger Evangelicals often did not speak or write German with any fluency, and pushed for at least some English in the services.

With hindsight, it is easy to say that of course the Evangelical Association had to make the switch to English. This was not so evident to all of those engaged in this issue at the time. To those who still thought and spoke in German, the change from German to English in their churches was painful and heartbreaking. The change was usually made very gradually, thus giving these people time to adjust to and accept English services, although some left and joined German Lutheran churches whose services were still all in German. The anti-German hysteria of World War I forced many churches into more rapid acceptance of English also, although a few maintained some German even in the 1930s.

Clearly, the change from German to English was forced both from without and from within, as it became more obvious to both clergy and lay people that the church would lose most of the younger generation who did not for the most part speak German, if they did not change to English. And while the change was often difficult and caused dissension within congregations, it is a real tribute to that generation that the transition to English was for the most part completed as gracefully as possible.

The decades discussed above (1891-1921) were fraught with

discord and dissension within the Evangelical Association. This was true for the Evangelical Association/United Evangelical split of the 1890s and for the German to English language transition which took place in Minnesota during these years. It was not a time of real expansion for the Evangelical Association, but rather one of dealing with major divisive issues. And while the scars from these divisive issues would remain for some years, what is more important here is that the Evangelical Association and the United Evangelicals reunited into the Evangelical Church, and Evangelicals in Minnesota were well on their way to completing the transition from German to English without major defections from the church.

The Evangelical Church: 1922 - 1945

These years for the Evangelical Church were peaceful and prosperous for the most part, if not for the world at large. With the discord and dissension of past decades receding into the past, the Evangelical Church was more able to concentrate on its real mission. The real challenge for the church in these years was truly to be "in the world but not of it," i.e., to be relevant to the modern age in which they functioned and to remain true to the gospel they professed.

The early post-World War I years were years of change and modernization, as new inventions and communications systems reached from the cities into the small towns and rural areas. The telephone, radio, electricity, indoor plumbing, etc., and perhaps most of all the automobile, were no longer oddities but were becoming commonplace. This meant that the church had to compete with many other available activities. "Keeping the Sabbath" as Evangelicals had historically done by attendance at one or more services and not engaging in "frivolous activities" was more challenged by Sunday movies, baseball or other entertainment not previously accessible. Other more "worldly" activities also became more prevalent and accessible, such as smoking and social dancing. These, along with drinking which had always been a major disapproved behavior for Evangelicals, were castigated as unworthy and harmful for Evangelical Christians.

But while the Evangelical Church was negative about what they believed were destructive behaviors, and worried about "humanistic" influences in education, they were also espousing a social gospel which recognized Christian responsibility socially as well as individually. Evangelical leadership spoke out against war and for cooperation among nations, and even with the advent of Word War II the rights of conscientious objectors were upheld by the church. The Evangelical Church continued to grow and change during these years between the world wars, and actions leading to union with the United Brethren Church would culminate in the 1946 union of the two churches.

The Evangelical Church in Minnesota during these years saw new churches in both Minneapolis (Oakland Avenue) and St. Paul (Calvary), plus a new effort in Duluth (Chester Park). Some of the churches on the prairie built new, larger edifices during this time; these were primarily churches located in towns. Most of the rural churches were certainly holding their own during this time, although declining population in western Minnesota resulted in the closure of two rural churches (Salem near Bellingham and

Fairfield Zion). This trend would accelerate in the post World War II years.

The importance of the establishment in 1922 and subsequent growth of the Lake Koronis Assembly Grounds in Minnesota cannot be over-estimated. Camp meetings had always played an important role in Evangelical life, and the Assembly Grounds near Paynesville provided Evangelical Minnesotans with a real Evangelical center. It would be difficult to quantify what Koronis meant to Minnesota Evangelicals both individually and collectively. It was a place where many young people responded to the call of the ministry, where God became a living presence in peoples' lives and where on "Koronis Sunday" the Evangelical fellowship of family and friends was not soon forgotten.

The Evangelical United Brethren Church: 1946-1968

The 1946 union which resulted in the new Evangelical United Brethren Church was carried out gradually. In Minnesota the two conferences actually united in 1951. The impact of this union was far greater for former United Brethren in Minnesota since in 1951 they were outnumbered 12,097 to 2,235 by former Evangelicals, but the union was a successful one.

The major issue facing the E.U.B.'s nationally and in Minnesota in these post-World War II years was the decline in rural population and the rapid growth of the suburbs. Since the Evangelicals and now E.U.B.'s had historically concentrated in small towns and rural areas, the new population shifts called for new emphases in the E.U.B. mission.

Conference leadership in Minnesota recognized the need for

199

an E.U.B. witness in the Twin Cities' suburbs and other areas of growth, and an ambitious missionary expansion program was launched. Seven new mission churches were established in the Twin Cities' suburbs and one in Rochester, between 1949 and 1968; this was a remarkable achievement. There were sometimes "outside" problems regarding location or other issues, and sometimes "inside" problems, with lack of enthusiasm and support from some E.U.B.'s in outstate Minnesota.

The post-World War II 1940s and 1950s also saw a great increase in church membership nationally. This was true for E.U.B's in Minnesota, and even with the population shift into the suburbs, most rural and small town churches continued to thrive. Some of the rural Minnesota prairie churches united with nearby larger churches (Clifton Bethel with Marshall Salem in 1947, Dunbar Zion with Wells Salem in 1954, and Brush Creek Tabor with Rice Lake Emmanuel in 1957), but these unions were not born out of drastic declines in rural church membership. These were years of optimism and expanding programs for most E.U.B. churches, but there were increasing signs that the religious revival of the post-war years would not continue.

The 1960s were years of change and often turmoil throughout the country. Some of the turmoil was destructive, while some was aimed at creating a just society where equal opportunity and peace could be enjoyed by all. Old ways and established organizations/institutions were questioned and sometimes believed to be irrelevant, hopelessly out of date or too authoritarian. The church was not immune from these ideas, and church membership leveled off or sometimes declined in many denominations, both large and small.

200

This was the case in Minnesota as elsewhere. Also, E.U.B.'s were more affected by increasing population decline in rural areas than were many other denominations who were more city-oriented. In Minnesota, E.U.B. membership went from 15,453 in 1960 to 15,289 in 1968. Decline in membership was largely in rural areas, particularly in far western Minnesota. Two churches on Minnesota's western border closed in the 1960s; these were Luverne (Pleasant View) Ebenezer, whose relocation into town in 1955 was not a success, and Yellowbank Emmanuel, which united with the Odessa congregation to form Odessa Hope. A movement to form a multi-denominational cooperative parish was begun in western Minnesota in the late 1960s which later took form as the Headwaters Parish.

But while there was some decline in some areas of Minnesota, there was E.U.B. growth in others, primarily in the Twin Cities' suburbs. Three mission churches had been started between 1949 and 1958, and five more were established during the 1960s. These eight mission churches accounted for almost one-tenth of the state-wide E.U.B. membership in 1968,[4] but their real significance was not in numbers. Their real significance was in their having been established by a relatively small conference with limited resources and some opposition from within and without. This move into the suburbs was not seen by Conference leadership as a lessening of its commitment to small town and rural churches, but rather as a commitment to follow people in their post-war move to the suburbs just as the early Evangelicals had followed the German immigrants into Minnesota one hundred years earlier.

General concerns about societal issues, declining church membership, and fewer ministerial candidates were present in Minnesota as well as on the national level in the 1960s. But the major issue for E.U.B.'s in the 1960s was the rapidly increasing pressure for merger with the Methodist Church. National church leadership for the most part espoused union as moving toward God's will that the Church be One, that real ecumenicity demanded such a union, and that the times made union expedient and necessary.

These beliefs were not universal however. Views were expressed that the proposed "union" would in fact be a "merger" in which E.U.B.'s joined the Methodist Church and that ecumenicity did not demand merger or union. Real "grass roots" sentiment for union/merger did not seem to be present on any widespread enthusiastic basis, and many felt that more information on the issue needed to be disseminated. Taking time to thoroughly explore and thoughtfully discuss the issue was also felt to be necessary.

Between 1964 and 1966 there were efforts made to get the issue before both clergy and lay people on a more widespread basis. The timetable proposed by church leadership proceeded, as the General Conferences for both denominations voted for union in 1966 and the Plan of Union received sufficient support to pass in 1967. The Uniting Conference then took place in April 1968, and the United Methodist Church became the voice of not only Methodists but former Evangelical United Brethren as well.

Minnesota Evangelical/E.U.B. Reflections

It should be understood here that the reflections which follow are not based on a scientific survey in which sample groups of former E.U.B.'s and former Methodists were all interviewed and asked to answer specific questions. Nor should these reflections be seen as a scholarly attempt to balance the benefits or gains of the E.U.B. merger with the Methodists against the detriments or losses incurred by that merger.

Rather, what follows is a summing up of the feelings expressed by the many former E.U.B.'s, both clergy and lay people, who were interviewed for this study between 1994 and 1998. Clergy included some who were not formerly E.U.B. but were serving churches in the study area, as well as several former E.U.B.'s who had served former E.U.B. churches and/or were now serving United Methodist churches in Minnesota..

Far more lay people than clergy were interviewed, and these lay people were overwhelmingly from the churches in the three areas studied. Many of the lay people interviewed were now older people who had been active adult E.U.B.'s at the time of merger; others were now middle-aged who had been young adults when merger occurred. They were, with only a few exceptions, now active United Methodists and not disaffected E.U.B.'s who had left and joined other denominations. Clearly also, lay people who were interviewed were people who felt strongly enough about their Evangelical/E.U.B. heritage and their current status as United Methodists to take the time to discuss these issues.

As people reflected on what their Evangelical/E.U.B. roots and heritage meant to them, a recurring concern was expressed

203

that this heritage would soon be gone. They realized that the merger had resulted in a church with an overwhelmingly Methodist heritage, but were saddened by the virtual disappearance of the names Albright, Otterbein and Evangelical United Brethren in their United Methodist churches and literature.

It was noted that former Methodist clergy and lay people often did not seem to be interested in or knowledgeable about E.U.B.'s and their heritage, but yet assumed that former E.U.B.'s should and would be well informed on the Methodist heritage. A former E.U.B., and now United Methodist church organist, illustrates this quite well, stating that once when he was given the selected hymns for the Sunday service, he told the minister (who was a former Methodist) that he was unfamiliar with one of the hymns. The minister was surprised at this, and said so, since, after all, this hymn had been written by Wesley. The organist was not being entirely facetious, when he then asked: "and who was Wesley?" The ironic humor here should only reinforce the belief expressed by many former E.U.B.'s that their heritage is but a footnote in Methodist history and not a living, breathing, if small, strand of vital United Methodism.

Some of the former E.U.B.'s also brought up issues related to E.U.B theology, spiritual concerns and moral values. There was some feeling that the E.U.B. Church had been more conservative theologically, and more openly concerned about spiritual values and moral codes than the Methodist Church. These people felt strongly about and supported the E.U.B. emphasis on evangelism and the maintenance of unambiguous moral codes regarding alcohol, tobacco, gambling, etc. They also stressed the commitment of E.U.B.'s to their church in both time and money; with regard to the latter, E.U.B.'s did give about $15 more per person than did Methodists at the time of the merger.[5]

Certainly the concerns discussed above were not equally important to all of the former E.U.B.'s interviewed, and there was widespread acknowledgement that change would have affected the E.U.B.'s if they had remained a separate denomination in ways that may or may not have been supported by all E.U.B.'s. For example, both clergy and lay people expressed concern that too many ministers now seemed to consider the ministry as more a professional career than a calling, but were relating this more to the times than to their denomination.

There was also acknowledgement that there had always been differences of belief and opinions on issues within the Evangelical/E.U.B. Church throughout its history, along with more pronounced differences from the other denominations. There seemed to be a feeling expressed with regard to the latter, however, that most Methodists did not see the E.U.B.'s as having been different but simply as another branch of Methodism that was now grafted back onto the family tree.

This did not sit well with some former E.U.B.'s who felt that the differences had been more pronounced. As one of them said: "We just seem to be a different breed of people!" Many of these people did not mind being different and part of a small denomination. As one E.U.B. stated at the time of merger; "my German Evangelical grandmother always talked about the 'verdamt Methodiste' (damned Methodists) and now I are one!" This may be a humorous exaggeration, but it surely gets the point across that many E.U.B.'s saw their church as quite different from the Methodists and felt that their church's theology and value system were distinct and worthy of preservation.

In reflecting on what being an Evangelical/E.U.B. meant, perhaps the issue raised most frequently was a feeling of the loss of a close-knit fellowship. Many people stated that they felt that the E.U.B.'s had been "swallowed up" by the Methodists and that they had lost the sense of a "family" church. They missed the national and state E.U.B. publications (*Telescope Messenger/ Church and Home and News Review*) in which they could read about people they knew or had heard of and could feel they had a voice in the larger issues of their church. Clear connection to church leaders was also missed; for example, a kinship with and deep respect for a leader like Bishop E. W. Praetorius was recalled and missed by former E.U.B.'s.[6] Many people did not now know much about their church's leaders and did not now subscribe to similar United Methodist publications, because they felt no real connection to the people and events reported in these publications. Many also noted the lack of close ties to the former E.U.B. colleges and seminaries (primarily North Central College in Naperville, Illinois, Westmar College in LeMars, Iowa and Evangelical Theological Seminary in Naperville, Illinois). They were particularly saddened by the withdrawal of United Methodist support and subsequent closure of Westmar College in 1997.

As has been discussed in earlier chapters, Lake Koronis Assembly Grounds was for many Minnesota Evangelicals and then E.U.B.'s a visible manifestation of the ties that bound them together as a church family. This concept was brought up by many former E.U.B.'s as they discussed what being Evangelicals/E.U.B.'s had meant to them. It was clear that Koronis was much more than just a place to them, and that Koronis had helped to identify and define who they were within the Evangelical/E.U.B. church family and the larger world as well. The virtual loss of Koronis as this kind of center both saddened and perplexed them.

The issues discussed above clearly reflect many former E.U.B.'s concerns about the general issue of "large" versus "small." Some aspects of being part of a much larger denomination were seen by some as favorable, i.e., more opportunities for women, more diversity within the larger denomination, more programs for youth and families in the larger congregations, and more opportunities for Christian service. The preponderant view, however, was that "bigger" was not necessarily "better," and that in fact the virtues and values of smallness outweighed those that "bigness" could offer. These virtues and values were, as discussed above, not necessarily literal. Rather, they referred to a shared sense of identity and close ties that bound Evangelicals/E.U.B.'s in community.

In connection with these issues and concerns there was some feeling expressed that ecumenism did not require merger and that the broader mission provided by a larger denomination might well have been possible with continuing cooperation with Methodists instead of merger. Many former E.U.B.'s felt they had had no voice in merger/union discussions until after the fact, and some also wondered "what might have been" had merger not taken place.[7] This is not to say, however, that these people are living in the past. On the contrary, they are overwhelmingly active, committed members of former E.U.B., now United Methodist congregations.

Still Marching Through Immanuel's Ground

As was discussed previously, the feelings and issues surrounding the E.U.B. merger with the Methodists can best be compared to the earlier German versus English language issue within the Evangelical Church. Loss of identity was a major issue in both instances.

It must be remembered that the use of the German language helped define early Evangelicals both to themselves and others. Loss of the old language was thus traumatic for many Evangelicals, and was made more so by the fact that at that time it was generally considered "un-American" to persist in using one's "old" language. In recent decades there has been more understanding that people can be good Americans without their being pressured into totally discarding their old language and heritage which once lost is forever gone.

So too should it be with regard to the Evangelical/E.U.B. heritage. Those whose identity was Evangelical /United Brethren/ E.U.B. can and should be proud of their heritage, and should not have to feel (as one former E.U.B. pastor put it) like one of the lost tribes of Israel after the Diaspora. Surely it is not anti-United Methodist for the Evangelical/E.U.B heritage to be remembered and celebrated both within local churches and on a broader state and national level. For, surely it is true as is pointed out in an article ironically dealing with extinct species that:

To forget what we had is to forget what we have lost. And to forget what we have lost means never knowing what we had to begin with. That would be among the greatest tragedies of all. [8]

Along with the preservation of heritage is its perpetuation, and to honor that heritage is to keep its precepts alive in the present and future. The Evangelical Church on the Minnesota prairie may no longer be marching through Immanuel's Ground under its own banners, but it lives on in committed individuals and United Methodist and other congregations who continue to witness to the pietistic faith which gave it meaning.

Notes

[1] Kenneth W. Krueger, Letter dated February 18, 1999.

[2] *Ibid.*

[3] Behney and Eller, *The History of the E.U.B. Church*, p. 308.

[4] The three mission churches founded before 1960 had a combined membership of 900 in 1968; these were Minneapolis (Robbinsdale) Olivet (1949), Minneapolis (Richfield) Peace (1955), and Rochester Bethany (1958). The five churches founded in the 1960s accounted for 569 members; these were St. Paul (Inver Grove Heights) Mt. Bethel (1960), St. Paul (Lake Elmo) Hope (1962), Minneapolis (Burnsville)

River Hills (1964), Minneapolis (Plymouth) Pilgrim (1966), and Minneapolis (Bloomington) Normandale Hylands (1968). Thus these eight mission churches accounted for 1,469 (almost one-tenth) of the 15,289 E.U.B.'s in 1968.

5 Bishop Paul W. Milhouse, "I See New Opportunities in Church Union," *Church and Home*, May 15, 1967, p. 12.

6 E.W. Praetorius was Bishop of the Northwestern area of the Evangelical/E.U.B. Church from 1934–1954. It is safe to say that the vast majority of Minnesota Evangelicals/E.U.B.'s would readily have identified him as the spiritual and temporal leader of the Evangelical/E.U.B. Church in Minnesota.

7 Re: "What Might Have Been": Obviously it is not possible to know what would have happened to the E.U.B. Church if it had not become part of the United Methodist Church. It is interesting to note, however, what has happened to some of the other smaller denominations in the last thirty years. Membership numbers include the latest available figures, from the *Yearbook of American and Canadian Churches: 1999 Special Retrospective at Century's Close,* ed. by Eileen W. Lindner, (Nashville, 1999). For example, The Church of the Nazarene had 364,789 members in 1968 and 615,632 members in 1997, and the Evangelical Covenant Church had 66,021 members in 1968 and 93,136 in 1998. Many of the large denominations have continued to lose overall membership; i.e., the United Methodist Church had 10,252,958 members after the merger in 1968 and 8,496,047 in 1996 and the United Church of Christ had 2,052,857 members in 1968 and 1,452,565 in 1998. It would appear that at least some of the smaller denominations have an appeal by their very smallness that the larger denominations may lack.

8 Mark Jerome Walters, "Saying Goodbye," *National Wildlife*, December/January 1999, p. 38.

210

Bibliography

Oral Interviews (1994-1997)

Wells Salem/Dunbar Zion
Irene Bebler
Marvin and Viola Ganzkow
Grace Grunzke
Alice and Violet Kaiser
Sherman and Rosamond Miller
Dorothy Neitzel
John and Marion Redman
Mildred Sens
Donna Winter
Dean Wolf, Pastor

Rice Lake Emmanuel/
Brush Creek Tabor
Mildred Draeheim
Hazel and Mildred Schroeder
Orville and Lorraine Urbain

Blue Earth Immanuel
Edna Baker
Margaret Johnson
David Murray
Phyllis Olson
Howard Paschke
Helen and Herbert Reko
Marilyn Schaefer
Vera Steinberg
Nancy Steinke
Quinton Strack
Gary Verzalik, Pastor

Blue Earth Salem
Freda Berndt
Esther Eckberg
Nathan and Hope Sydow
Lyle Krumrie, Pastor

Fairmont Salem/
Welcome Emmanuel
Leonard Anderson
Mildred Blanck
Mildred Gamill
Lois Handevidt
Harold Jagodzinski
Dennis Lindell
Caroline Piltz
Lewis Stock
Shirley Unke

Worthington Emmanuel
George and Henrietta Doeden
Hazel Doeden
Clarence and Vivian Erbes
Lucille Krusemark

Pipestone Salem
Neola Dahlmeier
Pearl Eikmeier
Margie Friedrich
Gladys Roth
Ruth Smith
Eugene and Mildred Witte

Bibliography

Oral Interviews (1994-1997) – *continued*

Pipestone Zion
Lorraine Draper
Nyla Prinsen

**Luverne Ebenezer/
Steen Salem**
Elzora Ott
Fred and Laura Paulsen
Mildred Paulsen

Hendricks Zion
Agnes Christianson
Wesley and Bernice Kurth
Robert Neff, Pastor

**Marshall Salem/
Clifton Bethel**
Florence Maronde
Lela Paradis
Hope Peltier
James Pudil, Pastor

Madison Ebenezer
Sharrie Sather
William and Clarice Smith

**Bellingham Zion, Salem,
Yellowbank Emmanuel,
Fairfield Zion, Odessa Salem**
Florence Bombeck
Dean Dallman
Hazel Dallman
Janice Eifealdt
Dean Gloege
Alton and Bertha Hanson
Clifford and Elizabeth Hanson

Harvey Kidman
Lucille Matthews
Helen Ness
Luella Ninneman
John Rebehn
Kathryn Rien
Gladys Schake
Minnie Schellberg
Irene Steffen
Elda Von Eschen
Lillian Wendland
Elaine Shelby, Pastor

Pastors and Wives
Floyd Bosshardt
Richard Gist
Howard Krueger
Kenneth Krueger
Delburn and Lorraine Kurtz
Robert and Vera Painter
John Praetorius
Lowell and Alta Reinking
Sharon Ruhnke
David and Esther Schneider
Edward and Joyce Stevens
Gerald and Liola Walder
Willert and Mae Zahl

212

Bibliography

Church Records, Histories, Membership Information

Wells Salem/Dunbar Zion Ev./E.U.B. (Wells United Methodist).

Rice Lake Emmanuel/Brush Creek Tabor Ev./E.U.B.
(Rice Lake Emmanuel United Methodist).

Blue Earth Immanuel Ev./E.U.B.
(Blue Earth Immanuel United Methodist).

Blue Earth Salem Ev./E.U.B.
(Blue Earth Salem United Methodist).

Fairmont Salem Ev./E.U.B. (Fairmont United Methodist).

Welcome Emmanuel Ev./E.U.B.
(Welcome Emmanuel United Methodist).

Worthington Emmanuel Ev./E.U.B.
(Worthington Emmanuel United Methodist).

Luverne Ebenezer/Steen Salem Ev./E.U.B.
(Luverne United Methodist).

Pipestone Salem Ev./E.U.B.(Pipestone Salem United Methodist).

Pipestone Zion Ev./E.U.B. (Pipestone Peace United Methodist).

Hendricks Zion Ev./E.U.B. (Hendricks Grace United Methodist).

Marshall Salem/Clifton Bethel Ev./E.U.B.
(Marshall Albright United Methodist).

Madison Ebenezer Ev./E.U.B.
(Madison Ebenezer United Methodist).

Bellingham Zion/Salem (Yellowbank Twp.) Ev./EU.B.
(Bellingham Zion United Methodist).

Yellowbank Immanuel Ev./E/U.B.
(Odessa Hope United Methodist).

Odessa Salem Un.Ev./Ev./E.U.B.
(Odessa Hope United Methodist).

Fairfield Zion Evangelical.

213

Bibliography

Books

Albright, Raymond W. *A History of the Evangelical Church.* Harrisburg: The Evangelical Press, 1942.

Anderson, Gary Clayton and Alan R. Woolworth, eds. *Through Dakota Eyes.* St Paul: Minnesota Historical Society Press, 1988.

Behney, J. and Paul H. Eller. *The History of the Evangelical United Brethren Church.* Nashville: Abingdon Press, 1979.

Carley, Kenneth. *The Sioux Uprising of 1862.* St Paul: The Minnesota Historical Society, 1976.

Danbom, David B. *Born in the Country: A History of Rural America.* Baltimore: The Johns Hopkins University Press, 1995.

Eller, Paul Himmel. *These Evangelical United Brethren.* Dayton: The Otterbein Press, 1957.

Harmon, Nolan B., ed. *Encyclopedia of World Methodism.* Nashville: The United Methodist Publishing House, 1974.

Huelster, August. *Gnadenwunder.* Cleveland: Verlagshaus der Evangelischen Gemeinschaft, 1908. (*Miracle of Grace*, English translation by Louise Bloch, 1960).

Lindner, Eileen W., ed. *Yearbook of American and Canadian Churches: 1999 Special Retrospective at Century's Close.* Nashville: Abingdon Press, 1999.

Lunde, Richard M. *History of the Evangelical United Brethren Church in the Dakotas.* Grand Forks: Unpublished Master's degree thesis, University of North Dakota, 1959.

Nall, T. Otto. *Forever Beginning: A History of the United Methodist Church and Her Antecedents in Minnesota to 1969.* Nashville: Parthenon Press, 1973.

Robinson, Elwyn B. *History of North Dakota.* Lincoln: University of Nebraska Press, 1966.

Bibliography

Books – *continued*

Rose, Arthur P. *An Illustrated History of Nobles County, Minnesota.* Worthington: Northern History Publishing Co., 1908.

Swift County History: A Collection of Historical Sketches and Family Histories. Benson, Minnesota: Swift County Historical Society, 1979.

Utzinger, Albert H. *History of the Minnesota Conference of the Evangelical Association: 1856 to 1922.* Cleveland: The Evangelical Press, 1922.

Yaekel, Reuben. *History of the Evangelical Association, Vol. 1, 1750-1850.* Cleveland: The Evangelical Press, 1894.

Minnesota Conference Records

Minnesota Conference Official Record (Conference Journals)
Evangelical Association	1921 - 1922
Evangelical Church	1923 - 1950
Evangelical United Brethren Church	1951 - 1968

Official Journal and Yearbook
United Methodist Church	1969 - 1998

Church Periodicals

Church and Home	January 1964 - March 1968.
The Minnesota Conference News Review	February 1963 - July 1968.
Telescope-Messenger	Summer 1994 - Winter 1999.
The Telescope Messenger	April 1958 - December 1963.
Together	April 1963 - July 1968.

Bibliography

Other Periodicals

Methodist History, July 1987.

Minnesota Genealogist, Summer 1993.

National Wildlife, December/January 1999.

Reports

Reports and Proceedings of the 1970 Assembly of the Commission on Archives and History in the North Central Jurisdiction of the United Methodist Church, July 7 - 9, 1970.

U.S. Department of Commerce, Bureau of the Census,
Seventh Census of the United States, 1850.
Sixteenth Census of the United States, 1940.

Index

217

Index

Index

Index

Index

U

United Brethren Church, 1-4, 7, 9,
  11-13, 52, 58-59, 83, 104, 107-110,
  118, 123, 130, 139, 164, 190, 198-
  199, 208
United Evangelical Church, 52-54,
  56, 68, 75-76, 81-82, 84, 107, 164,
  191, 195, 197
Utzinger, Albert H., 66-67, 75

W

Welcome Emmanuel, 34-35, 40,
  60-61, 71-72, 96, 102, 116-117,
  129, 152, 154, 157, 176-177, 185-
  186
Welcome Methodist, 176
Wells
  Central Methodist, 172-173, 184
  Salem/Evangelical, xx, 32, 65,
    71-72, 84, 95-96, 102, 115, 127-
    129, 152, 157, 172-173, 184-185,
    200
Wesley
  Charles, 5, 204
  John, 5-6
Westmar College, 206
Wisconsin Conference, 17-18, 25
Wolthausen, C.W., 36
Worthington Emmanuel, 37, 39,
  61-62, 71-72, 96, 102, 129, 157,
  177-178, 185-186
  First Methodist, 177-178, 186-187

Y

Yellowbank Campgrounds, 42, 85,
  130
Yellowbank Emmanuel, 42-44, 47,
  66-67, 73-74, 77, 85, 102, 117,
  129, 155-157, 182-184, 187, 201